PORNOGRAPHY

COMMUNICATION CONCEPTS

This series reviews enduring concepts that have guided scholarly inquiry in communication, including their intellectual evolution and their uses in current research. Each book is designed as organized background reading for those who intend further study of the subject.

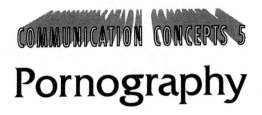

COMMUNICATION CONCEPTS 5

Pornography

Daniel Linz
Neil Malamuth

SAGE PUBLICATIONS
International Educational and Professional Publisher
Newbury Park   London   New Delhi

For information address:

SAGE Publications, Inc.
2455 Teller Road
Newbury Park, California 91320
E-mail: order@sagepub.com

SAGE Publications Ltd.
6 Bonhill Street
London EC2A 4PU
United Kingdom

SAGE Publications India Pvt. Ltd.
M-32 Market
Greater Kailash I
New Delhi 110 048 India

Printed in the United States of America

Library of Congress Cataloging-in-Publication Data

Linz, Daniel.
    Pornography / Daniel Linz, Neil Malamuth.
        p. cm. —(Communication concepts ; 5)
    Includes bibliographical references and index.
    ISBN 0-8039-4480-2. —ISBN 0-8039-4481-0 (pbk.)
    1. Pornography—Social aspects. I. Malamuth, Neil II. Title.
III. Series.
HQ471.L56   1993
363.4'7—dc20
                                                    92-46159
                                                        CIP

96 97 98 99 00 01 10 9 8 7 6 5 4 3 2

Sage Production Editor: Megan M. McCue

Contents

Foreword   vii
   Steven H. Chaffee and Robert P. Hawkins

1. Pornography *Is* What It *Does*   1
   How Do We Know Pornography When We See It?   1
   Pornography, Obscenity, and Erotica   2
   Sex and Violence   3
   Three Normative Theories   4
   Assumptions About Human Nature, Society, and Truth   6
     Theories of the Press in Society   6
     Authoritarian/Conservative-Moral Theory   6
     The Libertarian/Liberal Theory   9
     The Social Responsibility/Feminist Theory   11
   Pornography Research
   and the Three Normative Theories   15

2. Obscenity, Sexual Arousal, and Societal Decay:
   The Conservative-Moralist Theory and Empirical Research   16
   Arousal, Disgust, Habituation, and Promiscuity   17
     Exposure to Pornography and Excitatory Habituation   20
     Beneficial Effects of Limitations on Public Displays of Sex   23
   A Moral Climate of Laxness and the Breakdown of Society   25
     Prolonged Exposure to Pornography, Acceptance of
       Nontraditional Sex, and Leniency for Rapists   26
     Pornography Exposure and the Decay of Marriage and the Family   27

3. Erotica and Harmlessness:
   The Liberal Theory and Empirical Research   28
   Evidence of Demonstrable Harms
   of Pornography   29
   Contemporary Research With Social Statistics and Rapists   32
   Research Measuring Harm in the Laboratory   35
   Pornography May Be Socially Beneficial   37

    Individual Differences in Tolerance for Restrictions   39
    Research on More or Corrective Speech   42

4. Pornography and Harms to Women:
    The Feminist Theory and Empirical Research   44
    The Sexualization of Subordination and Violence   46
      Sexual Arousal to Rape   46
      Changes in Perceptions and Attitudes Toward Rape Victims   48
      Laboratory Studies on Aggressive Behavior
      Against Women   48
    Pornography and Discrimination Against Women   50
    A Cultural Climate of Aggression Against Women   51
    The Combination of Sexually Explicit Media
    With Other Variables   53
    The Effects of Pornography on Female Viewers   54

5. The Contributions of Each Approach
    to Scientific Research and Social Policy   56
    Unique Contributions of Each Approach   57
    Overlap Among the Approaches   59
    Returning the Concepts to Their Origins   59

References   63

Index   71

About the Authors   75

Foreword

Each volume in the **Communication Concepts** series deals at length with an idea of enduring importance to the study of human communication. Through analysis and interpretation of the scholarly literature, specialists in each area explore the uses to which a major concept has been applied and also to point to promising directions for future work.

Pornography, that is, sexually explicit communications, has fascinated and divided researchers, policymakers, and the public for years. Does it have harmful effects on individuals? What effects in particular? Does it affect everyone or just certain people? If harmful effects exist, what should society do about them? More than in almost any other area of social science, researchers have come to diametrically opposing answers to such questions.

Knowing that such disagreement often results from using the same term to mean very different things, we asked Daniel Linz and Neil Malamuth to help the reader sort out the different meanings and their implications. Our hope was that readers made sensitive to these meanings would be better able to understand existing research, to carry out their own studies, and then to communicate their results to others.

In this small book, Linz and Malamuth have gone far beyond our expectations, revealing a systematic interweaving of social science, morality, and the law. They describe three different perspectives on pornography—conservative/moralistic, liberal, and feminist. Each perspective has its own definition of pornography, each has a distinct research agenda with its own questions and methods, and each leads to different implications for law and public policy. That is, each of these perspectives integrates science, law, morality, and policy in particular ways that often pass unnoticed. While representatives of these positions have generally attacked one another, Linz and Malamuth are able to show the worth of each, deepening our understanding and appreciation of theory and research on pornography. Their success in revealing how science is integrated with the rest of social life should encourage communication scholars to reexamine the assumptions made about all research concepts.

Steven H. Chaffee, *Series Editor*
Robert P. Hawkins, *Associate Editor*

PORNOGRAPHY

DANIEL LINZ
NEIL MALAMUTH

1. *Pornography* Is *What It* Does

Communication science research on pornography in the United States is one area of the broader study of media effects. Investigators have focused primarily on how the thoughts, attitudes, and behaviors of individuals are influenced by exposure to sexually explicit messages. To understand pornography research, however, we must consider it in the broader context of the debate about pornography effects in society, especially in the United States. The terms of this debate have often framed the research agenda.

How Do We Know Pornography When We See It?

The question of definition always lies beneath public discussion, academic inquiry, legal decisions, and policy-making about pornography. Pronouncements by government officials about what is "pornographic" or "obscene" often appear to be highly subjective. For example, in an admission that has become a cliché, Supreme Court Justice Potter Stewart had to concede in one opinion that he could not define pornography, but he knew it when he saw it (*Jacobellis v. Ohio*, 1964). To say that the definition of pornography is subjective, however, does not mean that it is completely idiosyncratic or that there are as many definitions as there are peculiarities among people. There are several commonly shared points of view.

1

Pornography, Obscenity, and Erotica

The terms *pornography, obscenity,* and *erotica* have been used almost interchangeably in the pornography debate. Often, they are applied indiscriminately to the same depiction. This leads to confusion. In this book we view each term, and its unique definition, as a way of organizing three different types of viewer perceptions about sexually explicit material.

The term *obscene* is derived from the Latin *ob,* meaning *to* and *caenum,* meaning *filth* (Webster's New Dictionary, 1990). Indeed, obscenity has traditionally been associated with filth, and with offensiveness, disgust, shame, and the idea of insulting or breaching an accepted moral standard. *Pornography* is derived from the Greek *porne* meaning *whore* and *graphein,* meaning to write. Pornography, then, literally means the "writings of harlots" or "depictions of acts of prostitutes" (Webster's, 1990). *Erotica* is derived from the name of the Greek god *Eros* and refers to sexual love. It is often used to refer to literary or artistic works that have a sexual quality or theme.[1]

Each definition represents a different perspective that could be applied to the same depiction. A message may be pornographic to some viewers but not obscene. Similarly, what is obscene to some will be erotic to others, depending on what one emphasizes.

Imagine a photo layout featuring a nude woman with an accompanying text stating that the woman has had enjoyable sexual relations with many partners and that posing for male viewers of this magazine is thrilling for her. (Such a depiction might easily be found in mainstream U.S. magazines such as *Playboy* or *Penthouse.*) The photos might be considered pornographic by the definition above, because for some viewers the layout and description may suggest that the woman is a whore. One might view the presentation of the woman as intended solely for the pleasure of a male viewer and find the deptiction more pornographic than erotic. In this sense, the viewer might feel that the woman has been portrayed in a one-dimensional manner, primarily as an object for the sexual pleasure of man, and thus, as the term *pornography* connotes, as a type of prostitute. The photos and description would probably not be considered obscene, at least in most communities in the United States, because based on contemporary standards of morality they are neither sexually explicit nor shameful and disgusting to most viewers. (This is not true of all communities, however. *Penthouse magazine* has, for example, been labeled obscene by the courts in Hamilton County, Ohio, [Cincinnati] and is generally not available in that community.)

The same depiction could also be considered erotic. To be erotic, the depiction would have to emphasize sexual love. This could be operationalized as: "mutually consenting and pleasurable sexual expression between adults" (Steinem, 1980, p. 37). A viewer focusing on the woman's reported happiness about appearing nude, and her enjoyment of the many sexual relations she has had with men, might find the depiction erotic.

Sex and Violence

These three perspectives can also be easily applied to materials that have degrading and aggressive elements, or even to materials that inextricably intertwine sex and violence. Consider the highly controversial novel (adapted more recently to film) *Story of O*, by Pauline Reage (1965). This novel is about a young girl (called only "O") and her entry into the "art" of loving. It espouses the philosophy that women, by nature, are inferior to men and should therefore submit to their every whim and desire, this being the only way for a woman to find sexual ecstasy. O falls in love with a male practitioner of this doctrine and is forced to undergo a series of sadomasochistic rituals before he will take her in. O is then initiated into a house of bondage where the women are playthings for the male clientele. No talking or complaining is allowed. If rules are broken the women are punished in the cellar with whips and chains.

Story of O, according to a reader or viewer emphasizing the obscenity perspective, could be said to remove sex from the bonds of common decency and morality in the name of false sexual liberation. The story distorts the idea that sex is a communication of love between two committed persons. From her first appearance at the chateau, O is stripped of her clothing and of her relationship with her lover. He is revealed as a betrayer and she is thrust into sex with groups of strangers, eventually giving up her lover and entering into a loveless relationship with Sir Stephen, who becomes her director and master. As she is stripped of all caring relationships, she is falsely portrayed as becoming happier and happier. The basic purpose of the *Story of O*, according to this perspective, is to arouse the reader sexually and to satisfy curiosity about sexual practices that are disgusting and abnormal. More broadly, the entire plot of *Story of O* could be seen as an attack on basic social and

religious values. Through such portrayals the story works to desensitize
the reader to immoral acts in general and makes a mockery of humani-
tarian and religious values.

Emphasizing what is pornographic about *Story of O* leads to a different set of considerations. Some writers see the story as the symbolic
slavery and annihilation of all women (Dworkin, 1974). O's initiation
into the chateau is in fact a ritual by which men strip her of her identity
by beating and raping her. All women in the book appear as domestic
and sexual slaves, but they are portrayed as happy in their bondage. O
is chained like a slave and gagged while she is whipped to ensure her
silence. None of this is presented as enslavement, but rather as a means
for O, and by extension, for other women to achieve happiness. O is
denied the right to touch her own body or to choose her own sexual
partners. She exists merely for the pleasure of men and is expected to be
sexually ready at all times to spare them any inconvenience in trying to
arouse her. In its essentials *Story of O* is no different from other pornographic films or magazines, which sometimes explicitly, and at other
times, in a subtly disguised manner, feature women as sexual slaves.

A viewer or reader emphasizing the erotic in *Story of O* might freely
admit that some of the sex is animalistic and violent. However, an adherent
to this perspective would probably add the assertion that violence is a
feature of sex in nature. Consensual, sexually aggressive practices such
as the love bite are natural extensions of sex in this view. Further, it may
be asked: Who are we to judge what is arousing and what ultimately
provides pleasure and release for other persons? The story is just that—a
fiction—which merely triggers sexual thoughts that are not acted out.
The practices portrayed in the *Story of O* can be understood as exaggerations of sexual tendencies that arouse without inspiring exact imitation.
The descriptions have an air of unreality, and may provide stimulation
in the sex lives of some people by means of harmless fantasy; no one is
hurt by these portrayals. Like many works of art, the *Story of O* may
even be sexually liberating for the reader or viewer, because O overcomes
her fear of deriving pleasure from a bondage game and chooses her own
pleasure over what other persons think she should consider pleasurable.

Three Normative Theories

The reader may have noted that our description of the three perspectives' treatment of *Story of O* was not a simple categorization of features

of the story within the confines of a definition. It included speculations about the *effects* of this portrayal on people who read or view it and on the larger society in which it is found. Hypotheses about effects, each different, follow naturally from each perspective. In this sense, what people *see* when they look at sexually explicit materials is fundamentally tied to what they think it *does* to others.

Three theories about the effects of sexually explicit materials—*conservative-moralist*, *liberal*, and *feminist*—correspond to the definitions of obscenity, erotica, and pornography. These theories have dominated the debate about pornography, but they often seem to talk past one another because they define the issues so differently.

The obscenity perspective focuses on the effect of sexual arousal in the individual reader in response to practices that are considered disgusting or offensive. More broadly, the conservative-moralist approach suggests that sexually explicit materials often attack basic societal and religious values, and the reader or viewer may become desensitized to immoral acts in general. The pornographic (feminist) interpretation assumes that harm to all women in our society arises from portraying a woman as happy in sexual enslavement and as existing merely for the pleasure of men. Furthermore, there are harms to particular women from men who internalize this message and act upon it. In contrast to both these theories, the liberal erotica perspective suggests that the story is harmless fantasy. Potentially a work of art, the story provides stimulation in the sex lives of some persons and may even be sexually liberating for the reader or viewer.

These theories are broadly based beliefs that include both predictions about effects and also prescriptions concerning how we as a society should respond to these presumed effects. These beliefs embody values that usually cannot be tested empirically. Consequently, each of these perspectives is most accurately described as a *normative* theory. In science, hypotheses are derived from a theory and advanced for tests that may prove them false. If the hypotheses are not supported, the scientist tends to discard the theory. It seems doubtful, though, that adherents to any of these theories would abandon the basic assumptions behind their theories if they were shown ultimately to be false. Yet, within each perspective a good deal of valid scientific work is still possible.

Assumptions About Human Nature, Society, and Truth

There are two basic sets of assumptions underlying these normative theories. These assumptions are important because they lead to the unique predictions each theory makes for exposure to sexually explicit materials; they help inform proponents of each theory about the harmfulness or helpfulness of the predicted effect to individuals and society; and they suggest a social policy for addressing these effects. The first assumption set involves the idea that it is important either to develop the individual—his/her human potential, pleasure, intellect, and integrity —or to preserve social order and the community. The second assumption set concerns the relative versus the absolute nature of truth—the extent to which rules for appropriate behavior are thought to be permanent and preordained—versus arrangements that can be negotiated between members of society.

Theories of the press in society. As a theoretical framework for discussion of these assumptions and their effect on the normative theories of pornography, we recall earlier work on *Theories of the Press* by Siebert, Peterson, and Schramm (1956). These authors argue that the press always takes on the form and coloration of the society in which it operates. This work examines the basic beliefs that members of Western society have held about the press in relation to "the nature of man, the nature of society and the state, the relation of man to the state and the nature of knowledge and truth" (Siebert et al., 1956, p. 2).

The difference between press systems around the world is really one of philosophy. Siebert et al. identify three philosophical types—*authoritarian, libertarian,* and *social responsibility.* (Siebert et al., 1956, added a fourth type, the Soviet style Communist theory, which was largely a refinement of the authoritarian model.) These three press systems share core features with our three perspectives on pornography.

Authoritarian/conservative-moral theory. The oldest theory of the press is the authoritarian theory. It can be traced to the authoritarian climate of the late Renaissance in which Gutenberg's original printing press was invented. This theory of the press prioritizes the preservation of an orderly society over development of the individual and emphasizes the idea of absolute behavioral decrees over relative values. In the authoritarian society "truth is conceived to be the product of a few wise men who guided and directed their fellows, not the product of the great mass of people" (Siebert et al., 1956, p. 2). Thus, truth is found near the center of power and the press functions from the top down. This theory of the press as the servant of the powerful governmental figures was universally accepted in the 16th and 17th centuries. The rulers of the time used the press to inform the people of what they should know and the policies they should support.

The conservative-moralist/normative theory is, fundamentally, the authoritarian theory applied to pornography. Guided by Judeo-Christian theology, it aligns itself along the absolute end of the relative-absolute truth dimension. To the conservative-moralist, presentations of sex are harmful because they fly in the face of timeless rules for behavior laid down by religious authorities who represent the ultimate authority: God. What was wrong yesterday is still wrong today and will be wrong tomorrow. Prohibitions against homosexuality, adultery, and promiscuity in the interest of preserving heterosexual fidelity, marriage, and the family reflect enduring and immutable values. In its extreme version, the conservative-moralist perspective forbids even the dissemination of ideas about such behaviors as infidelity and promiscuity. It does so because of the power of these ideas to tempt the receiver into moral transgressions against the word of God. These ideas ultimately undermine moral values in society, which should not be questioned.

The moral conservative often views life as a struggle between the potential to unleash humans' individualistic, selfish, and primitive human motives and the maintenance of discipline and communal values. Exposure to sexually explicit material, from this perspective, fuels an overemphasis on sex and individual sexual gratification, thereby encouraging illicit fantasies and acts and debasing sex and marriage (Gardiner, 1967). Many proponents of the moral perspective regard the primary purpose of sex as procreation. Conservative religious leaders in the United States have been concerned with almost any depiction in the mass media that elicits sexual arousal in the viewer (e.g., Falwell, 1980; Gould, 1977). Public displays of sex, whether they be consenting depictions or violent pornography featuring rape, are seen as harmful because sex is defined as a private act and its depiction may arouse consumers in ways that impede their ability to limit their sexual behavior to private and traditionally morally acceptable contexts.

When the sexual actions of many individuals in society are influenced by this message of permissiveness, moral conservatives believe that a change in the general moral climate is produced, establishing a normative environment of laxness. Such an atmosphere can lead to a decrease in the authority and stability of other moral institutions. This theory, therefore, predicts that exposure to pornography will harm social connections and moral judgments in general. It assumes that sexual relations have a profound effect on other important aspects of people's lives due to the relationship between sexuality and such areas as family structure and involvement with the community.

The conservative-moralist argues that society has the right to protect itself from the disorder and moral disintegration that result from individuals unduly pursuing their sexual self-interests. Permitting pornography in the community is seen to undermine society by encouraging illicit sexual behavior. The government has the right, therefore, to limit such forms of expression that may be sought by individuals when the moral order of the larger community is at stake. Legal statutes regulating pornography reflect this moral disapproval of pornographic material. The State's traditional police power is "defined as the authority to provide for public health, safety and *morals*" (*Barnes v. Glen Theatre, Inc.*, 1991, p. II). So, in the conservative-moralist interest of preserving societal morality and order, public displays of sex can and should be regulated.

The development of the obscenity law in England and the United States is the written embodiment of the conservative-moral normative theory of effects and associated rationales for regulation. The law originally assumed that the predominant effect of exposure to sexually explicit materials is the "tendency to deprave and corrupt those minds open to immoral influences" (1857, *Obscene Publication Act*). A few years later the English courts elevated this theory of effects to the level of a legal test in the case *Regina v. Hicklin* (1868). In the adjudication of obscenity cases arising since the 1857 law, the U.S. trial courts usually applied the *Hicklin* test in the 19th and early 20th century.

The U.S. Supreme Court rendered its first authoritative decision on obscenity in *Roth v. United States* (1957). The Court ruled that "obscene" material was not protected by the First Amendment to the Constitution. It defined obscene materials as those that appeal to a "prurient interest" in sex (originally defined as: tending to incite lustful thoughts, or the incitement of sexual desire and sexual excitement, later reformulated as a shameful, morbid, unhealthy interest in sex) and that are presented in a "patently offensive" way. The prurient interest component of the *Roth* test identifies materials that fuel an overemphasis on sex and individual sexual gratification and that may encourage illicit fantasies and acts. With the patent offensiveness requirement, the Court sought the legal regulation of sexual works thought to be offensive because of their portrayal of that which is repugnant or disgusting to the senses, filthy, foul, repulsive, or loathsome (Schauer, 1976). In short, classic obscenity.

The libertarian/liberal theory. The libertarian theory of the press arose in the late 17th and 18th centuries. According to Siebert et al. (1956), it reversed the position of the individual and the state assumed by the authoritarian perspective. In libertarian theory the individual is no longer dependent on authority figures for truth, but is seen instead as a rational being, able to discern truth from falsehood, distinguish right from wrong, and to choose between better and worse alternatives. Truth is no longer conceived of as the property of authority or as timeless and immutable, but as an evolving phenomenon. The right to search for truth is thought to be an inalienable natural right of humankind. As such the press is viewed as a partner in this search. The press, rather than being an instrument of government, is a device for presenting evidence and arguments for a public that is capable of deciding policy. According to this viewpoint, it is imperative that the press be free from government control. For liberal truth to emerge, all ideas must get a fair hearing.

The writings of 17th and 18th century philosophers are the basis of this orientation. Most prominent is John Locke and his notions about natural law and liberties (the rights of the individual to life, liberty, and property). Freedom of speech is defended as a natural right that individuals must possess if they are to achieve the full potential of their intellectual and moral endowments. Interference with this right is objectionable because individuals are thwarted in the development and expression of their rational faculties. Institutions within society should be shaped so that they will promote the unfolding and enrichment of the individual's human character. A classic libertarian does not approve of everything that is said, of course, but defends the right to say it.

The liberal theory of pornography is a direct extension of the ideals of the libertarian theory of the press. With regard to the absolute versus relative truth dimension, the liberal position maintains that the concepts of good and evil are culturally defined. It asserts, in effect, that what we believe to be immoral today may well be acceptable tomorrow; what is considered obscene today may be considered erotic art tomorrow. Even within the same time frame liberals would argue that what may be pleasurable and arousing for some persons may not be for others.

The liberal theory of pornography's effects emphasizes the individualistic end of the societal/individual dimension. The theory maintains that sexually explicit speech is a result of the fact that humans are naturally sexual, and that a free flow of ideas about sex may help people reach their full potential as individuals. Within this perspective, sexually explicit speech is generally viewed as a socially beneficial form of expression, one that creates a fantasy world built around a variety of sexual interests.

According to the liberal theory, when humans are given free access to a full range of information about sex they are able to make rational choices about what is appropriate sexual behavior for themselves (within the boundaries of their culture). Without this freedom to discover, individuals and society will be deprived of moral truths about sex and sexuality. As rational beings adults are seen as capable of choosing whether or not to be influenced by the messages they encounter. By giving individuals free access to the full spectrum of messages about sex, society as a whole benefits.

For liberals, this free flow of ideas is so valuable to the discovery of sexual truths that it can be interrupted only when a grave harm to another person occurs as a result of exposure to sex-related materials. Yet the threshold for harm must be set high to guard against frivolous attempts at censorship of ideas that are taboo now but may be more acceptable later. As long as the recipient of sexually explicit messages restricts his or her behavior to private actions such as sexual fantasy, or only acts upon these ideas with a consenting partner, society has no right to interfere. Government intervention can only be justified if a consumer of these materials infringes on another individual's rights such as liberty, life, or health. For example, if it can be shown that consumption of sex depictions is causally related to rape or other violent crimes, the government may regulate such depictions. No effect short of these direct threats of violence is sufficient justification for society to interfere with the individual's right to view sex-related materials and with the right of others to produce them.

The legal history concerning government intervention and sexually explicit speech is essentially one of forcing liberal modifications onto the conservative moral legal test for obscenity, particularly as applied to works of sexual art or erotica. Even as the Supreme Court in *Roth* was defining obscenity as material that appeals to a "prurient interest" in sex and is "patently offensive," Justices William O. Douglas and Hugo Black, prominent liberal members of the court, said they would have reversed Roth's conviction. Citing traditional liberal assumptions, Justice Douglas noted that the tests by which obscenity convictions were obtained required only the arousing of sexual *thoughts*, which in normal life happens frequently. Douglas complained that to allow the state to step in and punish speech or publication because the judge or jury thinks it has an undesirable impact on thoughts alone when it is not shown to be part of an unlawful action, drastically curtails Americans' right to free speech.

Throughout the 1960s, the *Roth* test was further challenged and refined to reflect liberal objections to the suppression of erotica. In *Kingsley International Pictures Corp. v. Regents* (1959) the Court found that a film version of the erotic novel *Lady Chatterley's Lover* (1968) was not obscene under the *Roth* test. The Court greatly expanded the scope of permissible sexual portrayals in *Memoirs v. Massachusetts* (1966). At issue was the literary work, *Memoirs of a Woman of Pleasure,* commonly known as *Fanny Hill,* by John Cleland. This novel contains descriptions of many kinds of sexual activity. In the Fanny Hill case, Justice William Brennan, writing for the majority, ruled that the prosecution also must prove to the jury's satisfaction that the work in question is "utterly without socially redeeming value." In the Court's view, the First Amendment protection given to "socially redeeming ideas" was sufficient to override the accompanying portrayals of sexual activity. Three years later the Court further broadened its notion of permissibility by striking down another obscenity conviction in *Stanley v. Georgia* (1969). In this case, the defendant had been found guilty of possessing obscene materials in his home. The Supreme Court ruled that the First Amendment provides absolute protection for the individual's right to receive information and ideas about sex. That protection forbids state inquiry into the contents of a person's private library. Thus the libertarian approach to erotica has become well established in American law as an antithesis to the conservative-moralist perspective.

The social responsibility/feminist theory. Recently, people have wondered if the free flow of ideas is really possible under laissez-faire conditions. Today it is not easy to enter the publishing business or to operate a newspaper or television station. Mass media businesses tend to be owned by large corporations, and media organizations themselves are often large and powerful. The press, as in the old authoritarian days, may once again be in the hands of a powerful few, no longer representing a diverse set of viewpoints for consumer selection.

Recognition that a few owners and managers of the press determine which versions of the facts people receive spawned the social responsibility theory of the press, according to Siebert et al. (1956). The idea here is that the near monopoly media businesses have an obligation (a social responsibility) to see that all sides of an issue are fairly represented and that the public has enough information to make decisions. The purpose is to serve the public interest, not merely the private goals of commercial publishing. If media corporations do not take on this responsibility themselves it may be necessary for some public agency to enforce it, a philosophy embodied, for example, in the U.S. Federal Communications Act of 1934 under which broadcasting was to be regulated in "the public interest."

The feminist theory of pornography loosely parallels the social responsibility theory of the press. According to proponents of feminist theory, the liberal theory fails to recognize that the dissemination of ideas is often controlled by the most powerful members of society. The "marketplace of ideas" spoken of by liberal individualist John Stuart Mill is, ironically, just that, a marketplace. Those with power and money, usually men, determine what views are aired (Dworkin, 1974). Freedom of speech, when it comes to pornography is, in actuality, only men's freedom to impose their view of women on society in th name of individualism. Women, who are relatively powerless, mostly remain silent or are effectively left in silence by the dominant male-owned and male-controlled media.

The feminist position, like the liberal, assumes that values and "truths" may change from one historical epoch to another. But the feminist approach identifies the locus of value change in power relations in society. What is considered *right* or *wrong* in any one period is determined by who is in power. Currently, men control our society, and the values that men define as important predominate. (Presumably, this would change if women were equally powerful.) Because power is unequally distributed in society, men are able to force on women their notions of what appropriate sexual relations between men and women are, and men are even able to shape how women perceive themselves. The messages contained in pornography of women as whores and as sex objects are viewed by feminists as tools currently used by men to maintain a culture of male domination and female subordination.

The feminist position emphasizes concern for community over the individual and for the welfare of society over the desires and pleasures of the individual. Feminists argue, however, that the traditional moralist perspective, with its emphasis on sexual explicitness, arousal and excitement, and its notions of offensiveness, moral corruption, and shame, is misguided (MacKinnon, 1984). In their view, the regulation of pornography should not be a means for the government to preserve public morals or maintain "decency" in the name of public disapproval. Instead, regulation should occur to prevent harms to women, which include sexual harassment, discrimination, and sexual assault. The individual rights accorded by the liberal perspective to ideas about women and sex must take a back seat to the larger societal interest of protecting women from the discrimination that may arise from sexually explicit materials.

The feminist normative theory suggests, consistent with the definition of pornography, that what must be addressed is the presentation of women predominantly as whores and as willing recipients of sexual abuse and violence. Feminists presuppose that by presenting women in these roles, pornography is demeaning and degrading to women. Further, viewing it may foster the attitude that women are primarily objects for the sexual pleasure of men and desire or deserve sexual assault by male viewers. For feminists, pornography (and many other forms of mass media) perpetuate a view of women as sex objects and whores and, generally, as second class citizens. This, they contend, will result in discrimination and violence against women in society.

Because pornography plays a large part in defining and hurting women, legal means must be taken to limit pornography's pervasively harmful influence. Women have only one recourse—to take legal action as a class to redress the harms done to women by pornography, including lawsuits to recover damages due to pornography's harmful effect on them. This is not unlike parallel legal efforts to force the press to be more socially responsible for damages allegedly stemming from other harmful depictions such as violence in television broadcasting (Linz, Turner, Hess, & Penrod, 1984).

Recently, efforts to change the legal system to allow women to redress pornography's harms have been undertaken. True to the definition, these new laws are called antipornography statutes, not antiobscenity laws. The purpose of these laws is to permit women to redress the harms done to them by pornography both as individuals and as a class of persons. In the early 1980s, a model ordinance was introduced in Minneapolis, where it was rejected, and in Indianapolis, where it passed and became law for a time. In this ordinance, pornography was defined as the "graphic sexually explicit subordination of women," which must include at least one of the following features in order for women to gain redress for harms: women presented as dehumanized sexual objects, things, or commodities; as sexual objects who enjoy pain or humiliation or who experience sexual pleasure at being raped; as sexual objects tied up, cut up, mutilated, bruised or otherwise physically hurt;

presented inpostures of sexual submission, servility, or display; body parts exhibited in ways that the women are reduced to those parts; presented as whores by nature; shown being penetrated by objects or animals; or presented in scenarios of degradation, injury, torture, shown as filthy or inferior, bleeding, bruised, or hurt, in a context that makes these conditions sexual.

These ordinances include civil penalties for any person who engages in the production, sale, exhibition, or distribution of pornography. Any woman could file a complaint "as a woman acting against the subordination of women." The statute also created legal remedies for persons coerced into pornographic performances, who have had pornography forced upon them in any place of employment, in education, in a home, or in any public place, and for persons who were assaulted, physically attacked, or injured as a result of an assailant's exposure to specific pornography.

Immediately after the ordinance was passed in Indianapolis it was challenged by a consortium of publishers and librarians who contended that (in violation of the First Amendment) it severely restricted the availability of constitutionally protected nonobscene materials. They also argued that the ordinance was unconstitutionally vague in not giving notice of what might be a crime. A federal district court declared the Indianapolis ordinance unconstitutional (*American Booksellers Ass'n v. Hudnut*, 1986), arguing (from a liberal perspective) that an ordinance that makes injuries of pornography actionable is unconstitutional under the First Amendment because it prohibits expression of a point of view. Further, the court ruled that the ordinance restricted speech that did not fall within established categories of expression, such as libel, fighting words, or *obscenity*, which can be prohibited without abridging First Amendment rights. The court accepted the premise that pornography may harm women and may contribute to discrimination. But it refused to carve out a new exception to First Amendment protection, holding that the "state interest (in protecting women from degrading depictions that may contribute to discrimination), . . . though important and valid in other contexts, is not so fundamental an interest as to warrant a broad intrusion into otherwise free expression." The U.S. Supreme Court has, to date, allowed the *Hudnut* ruling to stand.

Despite this setback, advocates of the feminist approach continue to attempt to change the law. For example, in 1991 a bill that allows victims of sexual assault to sue producers and distributors of pornographic materials, if they can demonstrate a connection between these materials and their injury, was introduced in the U.S. Senate. The victimization approach has also been employed by the Canadian Supreme Court, which upheld obscenity provisions in that nation's criminal code, declaring that pornography harms women and can be banned (*Butler v. Queen*, 1992). In sum, the feminist approach is just beginning to establish its legal formulation. Meanwhile, it has stimulated a sizable body of social scientific research.

Pornography Research and the Three Normative Theories

None of the three normative theories is, in its totality, amenable to being disproven in a scientific sense. However, the theories have stimulated research by making assertions that enable the investigator to frame specific propositions that are empirically testable. In the following chapters we will describe how each of the normative theories has guided scientific research on effects of pornography. We will report instances where a normative theory has influenced the formation of specific hypotheses that can, unlike broader philosophical positions, be falsified. In addition, we will show how the perspectives have influenced the choice of dependent variables selected by investigators from among the vast array of outcomes that could have been measured, and how the interpretation of ambiguous or inconsistent study results has also been undertaken within the "mindset" of each perspective. Normative theories have guided social scientists in their conceptions of what the effects of pornography might be. Whether there is evidence of such effects can then be treated as a scientific question.

Note

1. To avoid burdening the reader with overuse of more awkward terms such as *sexually explicit materials*, or *public displays of sex*, we sometimes use the term *pornography* or *pornographic* when describing materials considered from the *erotic* or *obscenity* perspectives.

2. Obscenity, Sexual Arousal, and Societal Decay: The Conservative-Moralist Theory and Empirical Research

From our discussion of the definition of obscenity, and the moral conservative normative theory that is implied by this definition, we may describe the components of this theory as follows: (a) to many people, explicit, public portrayals of sex are disgusting and offensive; (b) displays of sex are arousing, and this arousal, outside of monogamous relationships, may undermine these relationships; (c) by overemphasizing sexual gratification and sexual permissiveness, pornography can cause its consumers to behave in ways that undermine other traditional moral judgments about women and sex; (d) ultimately, society in general, and specific societal structures such as the family, may decay once these traditional judgments about women and sex are undermined. The socio-legal formulation of this theory, the obscenity law, limits public display of pornographic materials when two conditions are met: if the materials are found to appeal to a "prurient interest" in sex, and if they are presented in a way that is "patently offensive." [1]

A program of scientific inquiry about the effects of sexually explicit material guided by these principles would: (a) include an emphasis on sexual arousal as a driving mechanism and focus on materials that contribute to sexual excitement; (b) be concerned with understanding how viewer disgust with sexual depictions determines reactions to sexually explicit materials; (c) focus on exposure to displays of sex as a force undermining traditional beliefs about sexuality and undermining beliefs in the larger moral institutions in society such as marriage and the family.

Research conducted by Zillmann and his associates is particularly relevant to the conservative-moralist normative theory. In their early work, these investigators (Zillmann, Bryant, Comisky, & Medoff, 1981; Zillmann & Sapolsky, 1977) proposed the arousal/hedonic valence model. This model posits that two variables, excitement and delight/ disgust, are responsible for a person's reactions to sexually explicit stimuli. A major component of the research generated by Zillmann and associates is the exploration of the potential loss of excitement, and of disgust resulting from repeated exposure to graphic displays of sex. A consequence of this habituation is that viewers are motivated to search for novel means of stimulation. This stimuation could take the form of stronger, perhaps violent, forms of pornography (Zillmann & Bryant, 1986), or an increase in the viewer's permissive sexual behaviors. Most recently these researchers have recently turned their attention to the proposition advanced by the traditional moralist, that prolonged exposure to pornography fosters a lack of respect for social institutions such as the family and traditional sex roles for women.

Arousal, Disgust, Habituation, and Promiscuity

To understand the arousal/hedonic valence theory of pornography effects it is necessary to describe the research context in which it arose. A series of laboratory studies was conducted, not to test theories about pornography but primarily to validate ideas concerning human aggression. Within the scientific community, the findings of these studies were almost always brought up in the context of "what increases or decreases aggressive behavior," rather than in discussions about the effects of pornography. These laboratory investigations were concerned primarily with aggression by males toward other males and involved exposure to nonviolent sexual materials. These studies suggested, contrary to prevailing scientific opinion at the time, that there *was* a relationship between pornography and aggression (Zillmann, 1971).

One of Zillmann's primary research interests was the effect of pornography on individuals who are predisposed, or *primed* to behave aggressively. To anger laboratory subjects so that they would be instigated to aggress, the experimenter had them perform a task. The subject was told that his performance on this task would be evaluated by another student, who was actually the experimenter's confederate and who deliberately made some errors. Typically, the subject's evaluation took the form of written comments and included the delivery of electric shocks to the other student. Subjects were then exposed to the sexual stimuli. Following exposure to various film clips or pictures (depending on the study), the subject was given an opportunity to evaluate the confederate's performance. The usual procedure allowed the subject to believe that he could administer a varying number of shocks or variable levels of shock to the confederate. The number of shocks, or the average level (intensity) of shock, administered by the subject is the measure of aggression in these studies.

Several early studies found that when male subjects were angered and then exposed to sexually arousing materials, their level of aggression increased. In a study by Zillmann (1971), for example, male subjects were first angered by a confederate, and then shown one of three 7-minute film clips that varied in their tendency to arouse people physiologically. The first film, *Marco Polo's Travels*, was considered to be nonarousing. The second, *Body and Soul*, was not only more arousing than the first film but also contained scenes of aggression (a boxing match). The final film, *The Couch*, was the most physiologically arousing. It contained scenes of a young couple engaged in intimate, tender precoital behavior. It included scenes of female nudity but no aggressive content, implied or otherwise. The highest level of aggression was exhibited by those subjects who were shown the sexual film, not the aggressive film.

Zillmann proposed an explanation for this surprising result based on the notion of *excitation transfer*. This explanation points to the arousal properties of a film as the causal factor in film-facilitated aggression. When a person is predisposed to aggress, the level of aggression will be a function of the amount of anger arousal felt toward the object of aggression. This arousal comes not only from being angered by someone, but from residual arousal from other sources that the individual may label as anger. If some external arousing stimulus (like pornography) is presented between the time the subject is angered and the time he has an opportunity to aggress, the subject's dominant response (aggression) should be facilitated. Studies in which subjects have done arousing physical exercise (Zillmann, Katcher, & Milavsky, 1972), or have been exposed to arousing noise (Donnerstein & Wilson, 1976) or to highly arousing humor (Mueller & Donnerstein, 1977), have lent support to the excitation transfer idea.

Later, however, several studies found that when male subjects were angered and then exposed to sexually explicit materials they displayed *less* aggression. In a study by Baron (1974), for example, male subjects were either angered or treated in a neutral manner by another male. Before being given the opportunity to aggress against the other male, they were exposed either to pictures of a nonsexual nature (e.g. scenery, abstract art) or to photographs from *Playboy* magazine. When subjects were not angered, exposure to the sex magazine photos had no effect on their level of aggression. More interesting, however, were the results for the angered subjects. Instead of showing an increase in aggression, which is what Baron expected, subjects reduced their level of aggression.

To account for this reduction, Baron proposed that many men find exposure to mild erotic stimuli, and the sexual titillation they produce, pleasurable. It is possible, Baron reasoned, that some people enjoy exposure to photos of nude or seminude attractive members of the opposite sex, and the positive affect induced by mild erotica may prove incompatible with anger. This incompatibility of the two emotions would tend to inhibit aggression following exposure. This explanation was supported by several other studies (cf. Baron & Bell, 1973).

But what about the studies that found increases in aggression following exposure to sexual stimuli, or the fact that some people might not find sexual materials pleasurable? To reconcile these inconsistencies Zillmann proposed the *arousal/hedonic valence* theory of aggression. This theory, as it turned out, accounted for aggressive reactions following exposure to nonviolent pornography quite well. It is also remarkably consistent with the conservative-moralist theory of how pornography affects those who view it.

Whether intended or not, the arousal/hedonic valence model proposed by Zillmann and his associates centered on two factors that appear to be similar to the legal test for obscenity for the conservative-moralist: "prurient interest in sex" and "patent offensiveness." Obscene materials are those that incite lustful and sexually exciting thoughts and are disgusting. The corresponding scientific theory proposes that a combination of two variables, sexual arousal and hedonic valence (how pleasing or displeasing, inoffensive or disgusting, the depictions are), could explain why people behave aggressively after exposure to nonviolent displays of sex. According to the theory, these two factors combine to produce annoyance in subjects. The greater the annoyance or displeasure, the greater the aggression in the subsequent task situation.

To demonstrate the importance of arousal and hedonic valence on annoyance and aggression, Zillmann and is associates conducted several laboratory investigations. Zillmann and Sapolsky (1977) examined the hedonic valence of various stimuli. Expression of annoyance by subjects was significantly reduced when they were exposed to erotica they perceived as pleasant but nonarousing. More specifically, males who had been provoked expressed less annoyance about a mistreatment after exposure to pleasant erotica (both nudity and coital scenes) than after exposure to neutral, less pleasant fare. These findings suggested to the authors that when sexual stimulation is construed by subjects as pleasant, and when it is not associated with a high degree of sexual arousal, it can intervene to reduce states of annoyance and the hostile reactions motivated by annoyance. Thus, sexual titillation from mild erotic stimuli seems antithetical to aggressive reactions. In several other studies Zillmann and his colleagues further connected hedonic valence and arousal with annoyance and aggression (Zillmann, Bryant, Comisky & Medoff, 1981; Sapolsky & Zillmann, 1981).

Zillmann and his colleagues also made an interesting discovery when they compared aggression levels following exposure to violent and nonviolent displays of sex. They found that if the nonviolent display is disgusting enough to subjects, it will produce the same levels of intermale aggression as violent sex presentations (Zillmann, Bryant, Carveth, 1981). In this study, subjects were exposed to materials that were matched on both excitatory potential and negative hedonic valence, but that either included violent behavior (i.e., a man being whipped by a female) or were devoid of violent behavior (i.e., a depiction of bestial sex). The researchers found that exposure to the displeasing, arousing displays of sex, whether with aggressive cues or without, produced aggressive behavior at a level above that of the no-exposure control group. These findings, according to the authors, were parsimoniously explained as *annoyance summation*: "If exposure to erotic fare such as bestiality and sadomasochism proves disturbing (and it apparently has this effect on many young men), this exposure further motivates the provoked individual and thus promotes aggression" (Zillmann, Bryant, & Carveth, 1981, p. 158).

Although originally conceived as a way of understanding the relationship between aggressive and sexual drives, the arousal/hedonic valence theory of viewer reactions, when applied to displays of sex, illuminates the conservative-moralist's legal definition of obscenity (i.e., appealing to a "prurient [arousing, sexual] interest" and are "patently offensive"). Specifically, it suggests that these two dimensions, sexual arousal and offensiveness, are pivotal for a psychologically based understanding of what is disturbing and annoying about sexual depictions.

Exposure to pornography and excitatory habituation. Arousal/hedonic valence theory assumes that sexual arousal (excitatory potential) is of considerable importance in understanding reactions to sexual stimuli, including aggressive stimuli. But what about continued exposure to displays of sex? Would prolonged exposure to sexual depictions eventually result in a reduction in sexual excitement? If so, what are the consequences of this reduction? Zillmann and his colleagues have systematically investigated the effects of prolonged exposure to nonviolent sexual stimuli on what they term *excitatory habituation.* Their findings are, once again, consistent with the conservative-moralist view of obscenity. Consumption of the same, or very nearly the same, type of stimuli becomes dull and boring with repeated exposure. Massive exposure to common forms of sex, because it diminishes the excitement that it initially produced, fosters an interest in uncommon sex displays. Only uncommon or deviant sex depictions would be capable of producing stronger excitatory reactions. The mediating mechanism for discontentment and boredom with highly familiar types of pornography is excitatory habituation.

Excitatory reactions to almost all stimulus conditions diminish with repeated exposure (cf. Grings & Dawson, 1978; Tighe & Leaton, 1976). This phenomenon is commonly referred to as *habituation.* Repeated exposure to a particular depiction of sex fosters habituation of sexual arousal as well as habituation to accompanying general physiological or sympathetic arousal, as measured by heart rate or blood pressure (Zillmann and Bryant, 1984).

Zillmann and Bryant (1984) have hypothesized that excitement is often a "hedonically superior state." That is, when given the chance, many people will choose to expose themselves to certain forms of entertainment to increase feelings of excitement. Understimulated, bored persons are often eager to expose themselves to exciting fare, even if it is not intrinsically pleasant. For these people, exposure to exciting material has the benefit of returning them to a hedonically superior, and hence, desirable state: the more exciting the material, the more pleasurable the state.

Zillmann and Bryant (1982) found that males and females who were massively exposed to common, nonviolent pornography, and who had undergone excitatory inhibition, were later dissatisfied with merely suggestive sexual material when it was shown to them. But their enjoyment of uncommon fare (pornography with sadomasochistic themes and portrayals of bestiality) did not decrease. On the basis of this finding, and their theory that people often prefer excitement, Zillmann and Bryant hypothesized that in the long run, consumption of nonviolent sex materials should lead to a modification of viewer taste in favor of stimuli that are less commonly available. These might include depictions of bondage, sadomasochism, or other deviant forms of sex.

Zillmann and Bryant designed a study to explore the possibility that continued exposure to common, nonviolent pornography promotes consumption of erotica portraying uncommon sexual practices, including sex coupled with infliction of pain. Male and female undergraduates and other adult subjects met for one-hour sessions and watched pornography for six consecutive weeks. The sexual behaviors presented included a wide range of heterosexual activities including fellatio, cunnilingus, coitus, and anal intercourse. None of the programs contained depictions of sexual violence, bondage, homosexuality, or bestiality. In a control condition subjects were exposed to comedies taken from primetime broadcast television.

Two weeks after the exposure treatment, subjects returned once more to the laboratory. The experimenter announced that there would be an unavoidable delay. Subjects were then ushered into a room (described as the office of a research assistant) that was equipped with a monitor, a videocassette player, and numerous cassettes. They were encouraged to watch cassettes from this collection while they waited. Each cassette package contained a description of the movie. One set of cassettes featured common sex with no coercion or violence. Another set of materials featured bondage, sadomasochism, or bestiality. The amount of time subjects watched each tape was unobtrusively monitored by the experimenter. Those who had been subjected to prolonged exposure to common sex displayed virtually no interest in the common sex cassettes at this later date. Both males and females moved to materials depicting the less common sexual practices, females, however, to a lesser degree.

Zillmann and Bryant argue from these findings that regular consumers of pornography depicting common forms of sexuality are not likely to limit themselves to these forms later. When given the opportunity, viewers will instead consume material featuring less common practices including sadomasochistic and violent sexual behaviors. They attribute this shift in taste to curiosity as well as to excitatory habituation to frequently consumed materials. Pornography featuring uncommon acts stirs curiosity and is still capable of arousing sexual excitedness. The researchers assert "that as a rule, consumers will advance to extreme material" (Zillmann, 1986, p. 21). For young consumers this may be more a matter of curiosity than excitatory habituation. For older consumers, a preference shift toward violent materials would be expected because witnessing violence produces sympathetic arousal and will supplement fading excitement due to habituation to common (nonviolent) sex. In any event, these authors expect, from both the findings of this study and their theories about excitatory habituation, that "the consumer of nonviolent erotic fare is likely to advance to less innocuous material, (including sexual violence), sooner or later" (Zillmann & Bryant, 1986, p. 576).

Beneficial effects of limitations on public displays of sex. What are the implications of the possibility that exposure to pornography eventually leads to a loss of excitement and to consumption of hardcore materials? How might the pornography consumer regain excitement?

Zillmann provided an answer to this question in his testimony before the 1986 Attorney General's Commission on Pornography. He noted that his research had shown that prolonged exposure to sexually explicit materials produces a tendency to seek out more deviant and extreme forms of sexuality. He suggested that by limiting public displays of sex in pornography we can discourage the diminution of sexual arousal and thus discourage interest in deviant forms of sexuality, and ultimately discourage promiscuous sexual behavior. "Abstinence from pornography offers itself as a viable behavior-modification strategy for the regaining of the lost responsiveness. . . . The enduring physiological changes that result from prolonged exposure to pornography are, in all probability, not modifiable by intervention techniques of 'mere talk' " (Zillmann, 1986, p. 7). Only by limiting exposure to pornography, he argues, will we be able to limit the need among viewers to search for novel, and perhaps violent, forms of pornography due to excitatory habituation.

Maintaining excitatory reactions through restrictions on the public display of sexual materials may have additional advantages. These are predicted by the conservative-moralist theory and from Zillmann's research. Voluntarily limiting exposure, or prohibiting exposure through the regulation of sexually explicit materials, may preserve sexual arousal in marriage and other monogamous relationships. In this view, traditional and desirable institutions such as sexual monogamy may be threatened by exposure to pornography.

In his book on the connections between sex and aggression, Zillmann (1984) points to animal and human evidence to support the conclusion that excitatory habituation should be expected to lead to "a successive loss of excitatory reactions to the same sexual stimuli" (p. 193). He examines research that deals with habituation indirectly through the revival of lost sexual desire that is produced by the exchange of sexual partners among animals. This research suggests that in numerous species the sexually exhausted males' sexual activity can be revived by the introduction of novel females. Research with rhesus monkeys, for example, shows dramatic habituation of sexual response to familiar females (Michael & Zumpe, 1978). The introduction of novel females prompts sexual performance to jump back to initial heights. These elevated activity levels then drop when the novel females are removed and the familiar ones introduced. Michael and Zumpe suggest that many of the societal precepts and prohibitions concerning sexual behavior have been instituted to sustain male potency rather than, as traditionally thought, to protect men and women from one another. In modern Western societies, however, such protective devices have been discarded in favor of permissive sexual habits, including the proliferation of pornography.

Zillmann conjectures:

> This is the wisdom of sexual modesty. The breast is concealed to give it maximum stimulus power for sexual engagement when unveiled. The argument can be expanded, in fact, to include the concealment of genitals. . . . Man resorted to sexual modesty in order to prevent the habituation of sexual excitedness, or in terms preferred by Michael and Zumpe, in order to sustain potency. (Zillmann, 1984, p. 197)

Zillmann's beliefs about the psycho-physiological effects of habituation and his recommendation to the Attorney General's Commission that viewers limit their exposure to pornography to maintain sexual excitement are consistent with conservative-moralist theories of the effects of obscenity. This theory proposes harmful effects once sex is opened up for mass consumption. By making depictions of sex more available, according to this view, we diminish, or in the words of the moralist *degrade* or *debase* sexual excitement in our private relations. For the conservative-moralist, marriage and monogamy are the proper institutions for sexual relations. To preserve and sustain sexual excitedness in marriage it is necessary to limit explicit displays of sex in pornography. In Zillmann's terms: if pornography displays breasts, then the stimulus power of the breast in a monogamous relationship is bound to be reduced through exposure to women's breasts in sex materials.

Excitatory habituation to one's marriage partner can have "devastating consequences" for monogamy, marriage, the family, and society, according to Zillmann. Excitatory habituation to a mate may lead to infidelity, the breakup of marriage, and the destruction of the family. Limiting portrayals of sex in pornography helps ensure that the marriage partner does not become sexually bored and thereby feel the need to pursue novel partners. The intention of socio-legal proscriptions on sexually explicit materials through obscenity law is the preservation of sexual excitement in marriage.

A Moral Climate of Laxness and the Breakdown of Society

Zillmann and Bryant and their colleagues have also tested the moralist assumption that pornography fosters a lack of respect for, and belief in, traditional institutions such as marriage, traditional relations between the sexes, and traditional roles for women. They hypothesize that the use of pornographic material may lead to a general acceptance of sex crimes, alter perceptions and evaluations of marriage, spawn distrust among intimate partners, inspire claims for sexual freedom, and even diminish the desire to have children. In effect, these researchers have turned their attention to the moralist contention that pornography is causally related to the general decline of basic values in American society.

In his testimony before the Attorney General's Commission, Zillmann (1986) argued that even a cursory inspection of the contents of the typical scripts of pornography reveals that it

. . . dwells on sexual engagements of parties who have never met, who are in no way attached or committed to one another, and who will never meet again. The parties have no rules for their social and sexual conduct and enjoy sexual stimulation for what it is at no social or emotional expense. This portrayal clashes with traditional values concerning enduring relationships in which sexuality and reproduction are central. (p. 17)

According to Jennings Bryant in his testimony before the Attorney General's Commission (1986),

if the values which permeate the content of most hardcore pornography are examined, what is found is the almost total suspension of the sorts of moral judgment that have been espoused in the value systems of most civilized cultures. Forget trust. Forget family. Forget commitment. Forget love. Forget marriage. Here, in this world of ultimate physical hedonism, anything goes. If we take seriously the social science research literature in areas such as social learning or cultivation effects, we should expect that the heavy consumer of hardcore pornography should acquire some of these values which are so markedly different from those of our mainstream society, especially if the consumer does not have a well developed value system of his or her own. (p. 1)

Prolonged exposure to pornography, acceptance of nontraditional sex, and leniency for rapists. Zillmann and Bryant (1984) argue that exposure to nonviolent pornography fosters distorted beliefs about the frequency of nontraditional sex acts. Massive exposure to portrayals of women in pornography may also foster the belief that they are generally promiscuous. According to these researchers, these materials may even lead viewers to believe that many women are so sexually promiscuous as to tolerate rape.

Consistent with the traditional moralist theory of pornography effects, however, these researchers have not shown an interest in dependent variables that measure reactions to the *victim* of rape by men who have been exposed to pornography as have feminist researchers. Instead, the research concentrates on the sexual behavior of the male perpetrator of sexual violence, punishment for his moral transgression, and interest in other nontraditional sex acts.

To test for greater acceptance of nontraditional sex acts and for an increased tolerance of rape, Zillmann and Bryant (1982) exposed unmarried male and female college students to approximately five hours of depictions of heterosexual activities over several weeks. Subjects viewed films that depicted heterosexual activities, mainly fellatio, cunnilingus, coitus, and anal intercourse. None of these activities entailed coercion or the deliberate infliction or reception of pain, but, according to the authors they depicted women as "socially nondiscriminating, as hysterically euphoric in response to just about any sexual or pseudosexual stimulation, and eager to accommodate seemingly any and every sexual request" (Zillmann & Bryant, 1982).

Several dependent measures were created and administered to subjects after they viewed their last film. Subjects were asked to estimate the percentage of American adults that perform common and uncommon sexual acts, to recommend a prison sentence (in years) for a man described in a newspaper account as a rapist, and to respond to a set of questions measuring sexual callousness toward women (Mosher, 1971). Both male and female subjects in the massive exposure condition: (a) estimated higher percentages of persons involved in fellatio-cunnilingus, anal intercourse, group sex, sadomasochism and bestiality, and (b) were more lenient in assigning punishment to the rapist described in the newspaper account, compared to control subjects who had seen no films. Furthermore, extensive exposure to this material, according to the authors, significantly increased males' sexual callousness toward women.

Pornography exposure and the decay of marriage and the family. Zillmann and Bryant have also investigated the effects of prolonged exposure to sex displays on acceptance of traditional family values. They make the assumption that the nuclear family is vital for societal welfare. Yet, they note, the values expressed in most commercially released sex materials obviously clash with the family concept, and thus potentially undermine the traditional values that favor marriage, family, and children.

> The decision to have a child, for example, is probably the greatest responsibility a human being can accept. It amounts to restricted freedom and to enormous expenditures for a good portion of adult life. If sexuality is considered part and parcel of such enduring relationships, it comes at a forbidding price. In terms of sheer recreational sexual joy, these relationships compare poorly with the short-lived ones that are continually exhibited in pornography—those that invariably show that great pleasures can be had at next to no cost. Prolonged consumption of entertainment with clear messages of this kind thus must be expected to impact profoundly the perception and evaluation of sexuality and its social institutions and arrangements. (Zillmann, 1986, p. 18)

Zillmann and Bryant (1988) have explored the implications of prolonged pornography exposure on attitudes concerning sexually intimate relationships, marriage and the family as societal institutions, and personal happiness and sexual satisfaction. The experimental paradigm was identical to the studies described above. Both male and female subjects were shown either nonviolent pornography or control materials in hourly sessions over a six-week period. One week after the exposure treatment, subjects participated in an ostensibly unrelated project on the "American family and aspects of personal happiness." They were asked to complete a *Value of Marriage* survey and the *Indiana Inventory of Personal Happiness.*

This prolonged exposure study showed that viewing sex depictions fostered greater acceptance of premarital and extramarital relations both for the consumer and for the consumer's partners. According to the authors, prolonged consumption also led to greater belief that there can be health risks from sexual repression, these materials conveying the idea that restrained sexuality is unwholesome and unhealthy. The most pronounced effects were on evaluations of marriage and the desire to have children. Endorsement of marriage as an essential institution in society dropped from 60% of those in the control groups to 39% in the treatment groups, and subjects exposed to pornography also wanted fewer children than did control subjects. Zillmann and Bryant concluded that prolonged exposure to sexually explicit materials that are commonly available raises severe doubts in the consumer's mind about the value of marriage and its future viability in society.

Note

1. Both prurient appeal and patent offensiveness are judged in light of community standards (*Miller v. California*, 1973). The Court later explained in *Smith v. U.S.* 431 U.S. 291 (1977) that "contemporary community standards" must be used to resolve the underlying questions of fact regarding "prurient interest" and "patent offensiveness." Empirical studies estimating community tolerance for obscenity suggest that even in politically conservative communities the majority of citizens may actually find sexually explicit material acceptable (Linz, Donnerstein, Land, McCall, Scott, Klein, Shafer, & Lance, 1991; Scott, 1990).

3. Erotica and Harmlessness: The Liberal Theory and Empirical Research

From our discussion in Chapter 1 we may identify four assumptions made within the liberal normative theory: (a) Most sexual depictions merely trigger fantasies that are not acted out. These portrayals are exaggerations of sexual tendencies that may provide stimulation in the sex lives of some persons, and no one is hurt by them. (b) As long as the recipient restricts his or her behavior to private actions such as sexual arousal, fantasy, or enactment of ideas in pornography with consenting partners, the government should not restrict individuals' basic human right to free expression of ideas nor others' access to these ideas. (c) Since many explicit depictions of sex present mutually consenting and pleasurable expressions between adults, this form of erotic expression may be socially beneficial. It allows for self-expression of natural sexual interests. Many works of erotica may be sexually liberating for the reader. (d) Since what is considered immoral today may not be considered so tomorrow, it is best to leave regulation of sexually explicit materials to the marketplace of ideas wherein competing ideas about sex can be presented so that rational individuals may come to discover "the truth."

Consistent with these assumptions, social scientists examining the effects of pornography in the liberal framework have selected dependent variables that address the possibility of direct or demonstrable harms (usually actual physical aggression or crimes) following exposure to pornography. Research that demonstrates *harm* in the form of changes in attitudes, or of behavior within the confines of the laboratory, either is not conducted or is discounted by those operating within this framework. Laboratory studies finding a relationship between exposure to pornography and heightened aggressiveness in a contrived situation are dismissed as irrelevant because they do not demonstrate a harm that is sufficient to justify restriction of expression.

Finding little *acceptable* evidence that erotica, as a rule, changes behavior in an antisocial direction, prominent researchers within this framework have emphasized the potentially positive effects of exposure to sexually explicit materials and individual difference variables that predict varying reactions to sexually explicit material. Kelley and Byrne (1983), convinced of the harmlessness of sexually explicit communications per se, have attempted to discover why some viewers have such a difficult time with sexually explicit materials. Variables such as sexual authoritarianism, low sexual experience, negative attitudes toward masturbation, and guilt about sexuality have been investigated. The idea here is to differentiate persons who approve and disapprove of pornography. Attempts by government officials, or calls from conservative groups to regulate sexually explicit materials, are in this view, evidence of sexual authoritarians imposing their views on others.

Research has also been undertaken on the effects of "more speech" to remedy the potential antisocial attitudes engendered by exposure to sexually explicit materials. The assumption is that the most positive way to counter the potential antisocial effects arising from sexually violent material is to add antiviolence messages to the marketplace of ideas. Specifically, this research has focused on the development and evaluation of antirape educational programs (e.g., Linz, Arluk & Donnerstein, 1990; Wilson, Linz & Donnerstein, 1992).

Evidence of Demonstrable Harms of Pornography

The body of research sponsored by the 1970 *Presidential Commission on Obscenity and Pornography* in the United States was the first systematic academic foray into the study of effects of exposure to sexually explicit materials. The liberal normative theory of effects determined the questions asked and the dependent measures chosen for examination by the commission. Liberal assumptions also determined the level of "proof" needed if a case was to be made against pornography, adopting what might be labeled a criminal conviction model of "guilty beyond a reasonable doubt." The commission's researchers searched for evidence of direct harm. This search paralleled liberal reasoning that speakers are not held responsible for illegal actions taken in response to their speech, unless that speech incites immediate lawlessness (*Brandenburg v. Ohio*, 1969).

The commission concluded that there were no scientifically demonstrated harmful effects of exposure to pornography and recommended legalization of all forms of sexually explicit communication. This recommendation was consistent with the modern doctrine of free speech and the "harm" principle underlying it: that freedom to produce sexual communications should be protected until the state finds specific, demonstrable, and substantial harm resulting from them (Downs, 1989). With the release of the commission's report, the liberal view that erotica has no harmful effects gained ascendance, at least among academics.

The effects panel of the 1970 commission investigated public opinion about pornography, changes in sexual arousal and sexual behavior following exposure to pornography, changes in attitudes and perceptions after exposure to pornography, increases in laboratory aggressive behavior, and the impact of pornography on delinquency and criminal behavior. The centerpiece of the panel's findings (both studies most heavily relied on by social scientists and used to formulate the commission's recommendations), however, was a summary of studies conducted in the 10 years immediately preceding the appointment of the commission. It examined the link between what liberals term *erotica* and *criminal behavior*, including sex crimes.

The panel relied on two types of data: crime statistics and self-report questionnaires from various populations of known offenders. These studies found that in the period from 1960 to 1969, the availability of sexual materials increased almost seven-fold, yet the reported number of sex crimes by juveniles *decreased*. Comparisons of delinquents with nondelinquents showed that the age of first experience with pornographic materials and the total experience with pornographic materials seemed to be the same for both groups. While the effects panel noted that more systematic research on the effects of exposure to erotica on delinquency was needed, it nonetheless offered the conclusion that: "taken together, these data provide no support for the thesis that experience with sexual materials is a significant factor in the causation of juvenile delinquency" (*Presidential Commission on Obscenity and Pornography*, 1970, p. 226).

The research upon which this conclusion was based included studies of recent crime statistics in the United States (e.g., Kupperstein and Wilson, 1970). While sex crimes *did* increase during this period, the increase was smaller than the increase in the availability of pornography during the same period. Furthermore, many other violent crimes increased more than the crime of rape. The panel concluded cautiously: "Thus the data do not appear to support the thesis of a causal connection between increased availability of erotica and the commission of sex offenses: the data do not, however, conclusively disprove such a connection" (*Presidential Commission on Obscenity and Pornography*, 1970, p. 229).

Given the ambiguous findings in the United States, the panel relied upon research done in Denmark, which removed all legal prohibitions on the availability of pornography during the period 1967-1969. Studies on sex crimes in Copenhagen by both Ben-Veniste (1970) and Kutchinsky (1970) showed a reduction in reported sex crimes throughout the 1960s with fairly large reductions from 1967 to 1969. There was no evidence that these reductions in reported sex crimes were significantly influenced by changes in the willingness to report these crimes. The Copenhagen data were considered fairly strong evidence for the position that laws removing restrictions on the availability of erotica would not increase the rate of sexual crimes.

There was also research comparing men who had committed sex crimes with non-sex offenders and with the general population, in their exposure to erotica, and their arousal and behavior in response to erotica. Goldstein, Kant, Judd, Rice, and Geen (1970) compared a group of convicted rapists with a nonoffender and control group; the rapists reported less exposure to erotica, both during adolescence and currently, than did the nonoffenders. Walker (1970) found that non-sex offenders had their first exposure to erotica at an earlier age than did a group of rapists. Johnson, Kupperstein, and Peters (1970) similarly found that sex offenders' first exposure to erotica was at a later age than non-sex offenders. Both sex offenders and non-sex offenders reported exposure to similar materials, with the exception that sex offenders reported more experince with materials of a violent nature (whips, belts, spankings). Cook and Fosen (1970) compared sex offenders with other offenders and found that the two groups did not differ with regard to exposure to erotica during the 24 hours immediately prior to their crime.

Based on their findings, and upon data collected before the commission was formed, the panel concluded:

> Research to date thus provides no substantial basis for the belief that erotic materials constitute a primary or significant cause of the development of character deficits or that they operate as a significant determinative factor in causing crime and delinquency. . . . On the basis of the available data . . . it is not possible to conclude that erotic material is a significant cause of crime. (*Presidential Commission on Obscenity and Pornography*, 1970, p. 243)

Contemporary Research With Social Statistics and Rapists

Since the 1970 commission's sponsored studies, several researchers originally involved with that report have continued to investigate the connection between pornography and criminal sexual behavior (e.g., Kutchinsky, 1991). Earlier research comparing sex offenders with non-sex offenders and with nonoffenders found that sex offenders reported *less* experience with erotica than did the other groups. As adults, sex offenders catch up with other groups in their pornography consumption, but they do not report using it more frequently than others. One problem with the early research is that it failed to consider experience with and reactions to *aggressive* pornography. This shortcoming was corrected by a number of researchers in the late 1970s.

Applying sophisticated physiological measurements and sexological techniques, researchers were able to measure the erectile responses of convicted rapists and of normal subjects who were watching, listening to, or reading depictions of both consenting and coercive sex. Early results (Abel, Barlow, Blanchard, & Guild, 1977; Barbaree, Marshall, & Lanthier, 1979; Quinsey, Chaplin, & Varney, 1981) appeared to indicate that normal subjects showed greater arousal to scenes of mutually consenting sex than they did to similar scenes involving coerced sex. Rapists, on the other hand, appeared to be equally aroused by the consensual and the coerced scenes. Subsequent attempts to replicate these effects however, have met with mixed success. Some studies have shown that among rapists, arousal to forced sex was significantly *lower* than it was to consenting sex; others have shown that rapists did not differ in this regard from groups of ordinary men (Baxter, Marshall, Barbaree, Davidson, & Malcom, 1984; Marshall & Barbaree, 1984).

Kutchinsky (1991) interprets these inconclusive findings as an indication that reactions to pornography have no consistent bearing on coercive sexual behavior, past or future. The research provides further evidence, according to Kutchinsky, that pornography is related to fantasy, not to action—an interpretation consistent with the liberal theory of effects. In the absence of solid behavioral evidence from physiological reaction studies, the only other "valid" answer to the question of pornography's harmfulness, according to Kutchinsky (1991), is the demonstration of a relationship between the availability of increasingly hardcore pornography, including aggressive pornography, and a growth in the number of rapes. Without this correlation as a first step, the assumption of a causal relationship between pornography's harmful effects, at least in the terms of harm as defined by liberal criteria, could not be scientifically proven.

To test the hypothesis of a connection between pornography and rape, Kutchinsky (1991) examined (as he had for the 1970 commission) the incidence of rape in several different societies where pornography had become readily available. He included 20 years of crime data in his study and assumed that a substantial number of people had been exposed to aggressive pornography due to a general trend toward greater public availability of sexually explicit materials of all forms. He then counted the number of cases of rape and aggravated assault in Denmark, Sweden, West Germany, and the United States from 1964 to 1984. The results showed that in no country did rape increase more than nonsexual violent crimes despite what we may assume to be a large increase in the availability of pornography in each country. In fact, in three countries, Denmark, Sweden, and West Germany, rape increased less than other nonsexual assaults. In the United States, rape and nonsexual assault followed about the same pattern over time.

The lack of a relationship between the availability of pornography and rape rates in four Western societies, including the United States, suggests that the widespread availability of pornography has not increased rape rates. This finding, according to Kutchinsky, is sufficient to discard the hypothesis that pornography causes rape. This leaves the debate where it was in 1970. If one were to base public policy on the findings of the research attempting to establish a connection between pornography availability and rape, the best course of action would be no action at all —a position consistent with the liberal theory of pornography effects.

Some feminists have criticized this interpretation (Lahey, 1991). They point out that these findings are contradicted by studies showing a relatively strong correlation between pornography and rape rates in the United States when the issue is examined on a state-by-state basis. Several studies (Baron, 1990; Baron & Straus, 1984) show that pornography and rape rates are positively related. Baron and Straus tried to account for differences in reported rapes across the 50 states in the United States. They developed several indices to measure state-by-state differences in rape rates. One of these was the number of copies of sex-oriented magazines sold per capita in each state. This index was calculated by looking at the sales (subscription and newsstand) of eight magazines: *Chic, Club, Gallery, Genesis, Hustler, Oui, Penthouse,* and *Playboy.* In 1979, there was a highly significant correlation of .63 between sex magazine circulation and rape rates. The correlation between rape rates and magazine circulation in 1980 was .55. A more recent analysis of rape rates between 1980 and 1982 showed a correlation with sex magazine circulation of .64.

Do the findings of this research indicate that pornography is a *cause* of rape? That is one possible interpretation, according to Baron and Straus. The evidence, however, shows only that there is a strong *association* between sex magazine readership and incidence of rape, not that one causes the other. There are a number of other plausible interpretations of what underlies the tendency for rape to be highest in states with the highest sex magazine circulation.

It is possible that a third variable may explain the correlation between pornography and rape. The authors suggest that a variable that might underlie state-to-state differences in both pornography readership and rape is an aspect of culture they label *hypermasculine* sex role orientation. When the authors introduced a measure of *Violence Approval* to the analysis (based on 14 questions asking respondents how much they approved of various violent situations), the relationship between magazine circulation and rape became statistically nonsignificant. This result suggests that attitudes favorable toward violence may account for both sex magazine circulation and rape rates across states. Baron and Straus believe that the *Violence Approval* index measures part of what they call *hypermasculinity*, or macho personality characteristics. Men predisposed to hypermasculinity may engage in acts of sexual aggression to validate their masculinity, and they may buy sexually oriented magazines for approximately the same reason. Of course, the reverse is also possible: that the magazines foster a culture of hypermasculinity, which also encourages rape. Correlational data remain causally ambiguous, and many social scientists prefer experimental evidence.

Research Measuring Harm in the Laboratory

Researchers operating within the liberal theory have tended to select dependent variables that assess evidence of direct harms (usually physical aggression or, even more convincingly, criminal aggression) following exposure to pornography. At best, according to this view, aggression measured in the laboratory is merely an analog to aggression and violence committed against individuals in natural social settings, and is therefore inadequate proof of a harmful pornography effect.

Consistent with its liberal framework, few studies were conducted by the 1970 commission on the effects of aggressive behavior in the laboratory. Tannenbaum (1970) found a laboratory effect on subjects who were angered and then exposed to aggressive pornography by examining the effects of various sexual communications on aggressive behavior (willingness of a person to administer electric shock to another person). Male subjects viewed an erotic film accompanied by one of three different audio descriptions prepared by the experimenter. The first description was purely sexual: A woman discusses an upcoming visit by her lover that focuses on sexual aspects of the encounter. The second description had an aggressive focus: The woman discusses her negative treatment by her lover and how she intends to kill him (poison, shoot, stab) when he arrives. The third version was similar to the second, with the addition of visual displays of the weapons she would use for her aggressive act. It was found that when subjects were angered, the two aggressive sex films led to the highest levels of aggression (measured by their willingness to administer shocks) among subjects. This study is now, in retrospect, taken as evidence that the combination of sex and violence may lead to subsequent aggressive behavior. However, the scientific panel in 1970 took little notice of Tannenbaum's findings, and the commission made no note of this laboratory study in its summary of effects of pornography.

Although not explicitly stated at the time, the fact that the commission ignored the results of this laboratory study is consistent with the liberal idea that laboratory evidence of aggression following exposure to certain forms of pornography is insufficient. More recent liberal critiques of the research conducted since the 1970 commission illuminates why laboratory studies of pornography and aggression are of questionable relevance. According to Brannigan and Goldenberg (1987), experimental studies of the behavioral consequences of exposure to violent or aggressive pornography are deficient on three grounds, all related to limitations on generalizability or external validity: (a) The aggression measured in the laboratory bears little resemblance to violence as it is committed outside the laboratory; (b) most experiments are conducted on nonrandom samples of college students; (c) the laboratory situation is filled with cues that guide the subject's behavior in unintended ways.

The typical social psychology experiment concerning the effects of exposure to pornography has the following form. Subjects are culled from a roster of university students enrolled in introductory psychology classes. Groups are then created by random assignment for different viewing experiences. In each group, subjects are first angered by a female confederate who very critically assesses a written assignment prepared by the subject in what is presented as a learning experiment. Later, each group is exposed to one of several kinds of visual stimuli (e.g., neutral, erotic, or aggressive pornography). Finally, subjects are asked to "teach" the person, who had angered them earlier by administering electric shocks for incorrect responses in a bogus learning experiment. The level of shock delivered by the subject is the measure of aggression.

The first danger of this design, according to a liberal critique (Gray, 1982), is that what is finally measured as evidence of aggression is an interaction effect of the stimulus on angered subjects (frustration and type of film). The fact that subjects are first angered may distort the effects of the stimuli considerably from what might be experienced by nonangered subjects. Unless we presume that real world actors are normally angry when they view sexual depictions, interpretations of the effects on nonangered others "simply are not defensible" (Brannigan & Goldenberg, 1987, p. 264). Other social scientists adopting this perspective argue that the ability to create or facilitate aggression in the laboratory tells us little about factors operating in the real world to produce assault, crimes of violence, or rape (Christensen, 1990; Gross, 1983; Jarvie, 1986, 1987; McKay & Dolff, 1985; Soble, 1986; Williams, 1979; Wurtzel & Lometti, 1984).

Second, liberal social scientists are concerned that the subjects of most laboratory experiments are not representative of those persons about whom we might wish to generalize. They note that if subjects chosen for experimentation differ systematically from this population, generalization is not warranted. Since university students in psychology classes are rarely exposed to aggressive pornography in their own lives, they are not a very appropriate group to examine for the effects such materials might have on voluntary, habitual consumers of pornography.

Third, liberals assert that the laboratory experimenter gives subtle cues to subjects from which a response is constructed; these cues are usually inadvertent (Orne, 1962; Rosenthal & Rosnow, 1969; Rosenwald, 1986). Such demand characteristics also arise from the limitations or confinement of responses imposed by the procedure. In the usual pornography experiment, the only response allowed is the administration of shock to the confederate. No other response is allowed (i.e., no positive response, no constructive opposition). All shocks are construed as aggression, even though the subject is told that it is a learning experiment, and that shocks are encouraged to enhance learning. Consequently, subjects are drawn into a behavior they might not select if given a broader range of options. In a society in which responses to anger other than aggression are permitted, aggression need not be the main response of angered men (Gray, 1982).

In summary, according to Brannigan and Goldenberg (1987), in the "real world," consumers of pornography may not be angry, and pornography's possible effects would rarely be expressed via immediate opportunities to shock a confederate in a learning experiment where punishment may have an altruistic foundation and scientific legitimacy. In this view, the relationships discovered in the laboratories are so far removed from the circumstances about which we legitimately are worried, and the results are so qualified in terms of their equivalence to existing social circumstances, that they are practically useless. To these scientists, laboratory experimental data concerning harmful effects of aggressive pornography do not demonstrate clearly such effects, and legislation based on these experimental findings is unwarranted.

Pornography May Be Socially Beneficial

The liberal position also considers that pornography may be beneficial in allowing the individual to create a fantasy world built around sexual interests. There is the suggestion that pornographic materials provide a way of releasing strong sexual urges without causing harm to others.

Public opinion surveys conducted by the 1970 commission indicated that many people agreed with this assessment. The panel funded public opinion surveys of American adults (aged 21 and up) and of young persons (aged 15-20) to determine whether Americans thought the availability of erotic materials was a social problem. When asked about the effects of exposure to erotic materials on themselves, individuals were more likely to list effects the commission termed *socially desirable* than socially undesirable ones. For example, virtually none of those surveyed reported that it led them to commit rape or made them "sex crazy," while 24% said it gave them information about sex, and 10% said that it improved their sexual relations. Even in situations where respondents believed that erotica had negative effects, they assumed these effects happened to other people, not themselves. More recent national surveys only broadly describe respondents' concern about the pervasiveness of pornography in U.S. society (Yankelovich, Clancy, & Schulman, 1986). Studies of trends in public opinion on permissiveness toward pornography suggest a complex pattern of shifting levels of tolerance for these materials. Some investigators (e.g., Smith, 1987) conclude that support for government regulation of pornography rose rapidly from 1975 to 1977 and then fell between 1977 and 1982.

The sexual arousal studies conducted by the 1970 commission indicated that exposure to pornography tends to result in an only transitory increase in masturbation or coitus among those already habitually engaging in these activities. On the whole, individuals became less excited and more bored with continued viewing of sexually explicit materials (see also Zillmann, 1986). A study by Howard, Reifler, and Liptzin (1971) illustrates this effect. Men were first shown a sexually explicit film. During the following 3 weeks they were given the opportunity to view sexually explicit materials for 90 minutes a day, 5 days a week. In the 5th week, and again about 8 weeks after that, the men were shown the same sexually explicit film. Results showed that with the passage of time the men were less physiologically responsive to sexual materials (over the period of the study) and showed less interest in the materials (as measured by time spent viewing erotica). In addition, the men became more liberal in their attitudes regarding pornography. Following massive exposure to sexual materials, they felt that pornography would not harm adults or stable adolescents and were less inclined to endorse controls on the sale and distribution of pornography. The investigators concluded that "exposure to pornography was a relatively innocuous stimulus without lasting or detrimental effect on the individual or his behavior" (Howard et al., 1971, p. 97).

Experimental research done for the panel also demonstrated that exposure to erotica did not significantly change previously established sexual patterns. People who were sexually active before exposure remained so afterward, and those inactive before exposure remained so afterward. Studies by Byrne and Lamberth (1970); Davis and Braucht (1970); Kutchinsky (1970); Mann, Sidman, and Starr (1970); and Mosher (1970) all found no antisocial changes in sexual behavior after short- or long-term exposure to erotica. When married couples were exposed to erotica, normal sexual activity increased temporarily (up to 24 hours after exposure), then returned to normal levels. For people not currently involved in a sexual relationship, there was no evidence of increased heterosexual activity. There was increased masturbation in a minority of study participants (up to 30%) who already had a history of frequent masturbation. Generally, any increase in heterosexual activity following exposure to pornography depended upon the presence of a consenting partner with whom the participant was already engaged in sexual activity.

A few of the studies have also examined the influence of erotica on low-frequency sexual activity such as homosexuality, anal sex, group sex, and sadomasochism. Both a short-term exposure study (one exposure) and a long-term study (4 weeks) found no evidence of increases in sexual activity immediately or within 6 months after exposure to materials that included depictions of these activities (Mann et al., 1970; Mosher, 1970).

After reviewing these studies, the panel reached the following conclusion about the relationship between exposure to erotica and sexual arousal and sexual behavior:

> The findings of the available research cast considerable doubt on the thesis that erotica is a determinant of either the extent or nature of individuals' habitual sexual behavior. Such behavioral effects as were observed were short-lived, and consisted virtually exclusively of transitory increase in masturbation or coitus among persons who habitually engage in these activities. (*Presidential Commission on Obscenity and Pornography*, 1970, p. 194)

Individual Differences in Tolerance for Restrictions

Finding no evidence of direct harmful effects on sexual behavior among the general population, the scientific focus, based on liberal assumptions, shifted to individual differences and preferences. The 1970 commission found that exposure to pornography tends to produce more liberal or tolerant attitudes regarding restrictions on pornography. However, these findings occurred primarily among persons who were low in sex guilt and who did not have feelings of disgust from viewing the films. In other studies such as that of Mosher (1973) and Byrne and Lamberth (1970), it was found that nearly all subjects considered images of oral sex, anal sex, and homosexuality more obscene than traditional heterosexual intercourse, but this difference was most pronounced for people low in sexual experience and less educated.

Social science theory about reactions to pornography within this framework has also emphasized other, conceptually similar, individual difference variables, such as authoritarianism, low sexual experience, negative attitudes toward masturbation, and guilt and anxiety about sexuality (Byrne, Fisher, Lamberth, & Mitchell, 1974; Byrne & Kelley, 1981; Kelley, 1985b; Mosher, 1973). This focus on disgust with sex and similar individual differences has been fashioned into a theory of response to pornography known as *Sexual Behavior Sequence* theory. This theory is derived from Byrne's reinforcement theory of interpersonal attraction (Kelley & Byrne, 1983) and is consistent with the liberal idea that many objections to pornography stem from repressed attitudes about sex. The theory takes a decidedly "weak message" position. It assumes that to examine the direct effects of sexually explicit communication is deemed not useful; rather, it is the *interpretation* that a sexually repressed or a sexually liberated individual makes that is important.

Studies of persons classified as having negative sexual attitudes have shown such associated behaviors as avoidance of sexual situations (Gerrard & Gibbons, 1982) and poor retention of sexual information (Schwartz, 1973). People who express positive sexual attitudes would be expected to approach rather than avoid, and accept rather than reject, sexually oriented stimuli (Byrne, 1982). Kelley and Byrne (1983) have found that these dispositional variables are related to subjects' responses to erotica. Specifically, Kelley and Byrne have been most concerned with two individual difference variables: low versus high sex guilt, and sexual authoritarianism versus egalitarianism. The first bipolar concept refers to the tendency for people to rate their feelings about sexuality either negatively or positively. The second refers to either approval or disapproval of sexual stimulation, tolerance or intolerance for sexual expression, and a high or low desire to control the sexuality of others. Sexual authoritarians have a higher recognition threshold for sexual stimuli than egalitarians do (Kogan, 1956) and they recommend imposition of more severe sentences for the sexual abuse of children (Garcia & Griffitt, 1978).

Theorists in the liberal tradition hypothesize that the sexual concerns of authoritarians have led to the labeling of erotic material as bad per se, and to attempts at controlling others' access to it. Kelley (1985a), for example, asserts that most official restrictions of sexually explicit material in U.S. society are advocated by individuals who fit this pattern of high sexual authoritarianism and high sex guilt. Because, according to her own research, there are no negative effects for exposure to sexually explicit materials, attempts at state restrictions can best be explained as sex authoritarianism. This fits well with the assumptions within the conservative-moralist theory described in Chapter 1. We noted that this perspective emphasizes individual dependence on authority figures for truth and deemphasizes the notion of people as rational beings able to discern truth from falsehood, to distinguish right and wrong, or to choose between better and worse alternatives.

The conservative-moralist assumption that others in society are not able to discern the truth implicates another personal characteristic that may be associated with the desire to restrict sexually explicit materials: the perception a person has about the influence these depictions have on others. Gunther (1991) notes that public support for censorship of sexually explicit materials is often justified by the argument that such content has negative effects on others. He points out that while it is clear that people are concerned with such effects on others, it is not clear whether they are also concerned about effects on themselves. In a survey of U.S. adults, Gunther found that people systematically estimate that the effects of pornography are significantly greater for others than for themselves (an instance of the phenomenon known as the *third person effect*). More to the point, he found that those individuals who exhibited the third person pornography effect most strongly supported restrictions on sexually explicit materials.

The liberal position would hold that if the harmful effects of the materials are in the eye of the beholder, then, naturally, nothing should be done about the "problem of pornography." Calls for censorship of these essentially harmless materials have come from sexually repressed individuals who interpret them as harmful. Further, calls for restrictions by some individuals may be based on the assumption that unlike themselves, others will be unable to discern truth from falsity and will be unduly influenced by these materials. In summary, the liberals see such attempts by government officials and conservative groups to regulate pornography as the actions of sexual authoritarians who think they have the right to impose their views about sexuality and the effects of sexually explicit material on others.

Research on More or Corrective Speech

It is best, according to the liberal perspective, to leave regulation of sexually explicit materials to the marketplace of ideas. Competing and varying ideas about sex must be presented so that rational individuals may eventually come to discover the truth. Several studies of the effectiveness of subject debriefings following exposure to sexual violence in laboratory experiments (discussed in the next chapter) have shown that more speech, or corrective speech, in the form of educational messages about rape and the mass media, can affect viewer attitudes. Malamuth and Check (1984) conducted a study in which male and female subjects were exposed to sexually explicit stories depicting either rape or mutually consenting intercourse. Afterward, the men and women exposed to the rape version were given statements emphasizing that the depiction of rape in the stories they read was fallacious, and that in reality rape is a terrible crime. Subjects were also given specific examples of rape myths with assurance that these commonly-held beliefs are fictitious. These subjects who were exposed to the rape stories, as well as debriefed, were less inclined to see women as wanting to be raped and to see victim behavior as a cause of rape than were subjects who read the consenting story but received no debriefing. In a conceptual replication of this experiment, Check and Malamuth (1984) found that men exposed to a rape debriefing gave a rapist described in a newspaper report more severe sentencing and were less likely to view the rape victim as responsible for her own assault.

Linz, Donnerstein, Bross, and Chapin (1986) have examined the effectiveness of a *pre-film message* informing male viewers who were later exposed to several R-rated "slasher" films. These films portray violence against women, often juxtaposed with mildly erotic sexual content. Prefilm messages were devised suggesting to the men that negative psychological effects might result from viewing this form of sexually violent media—specifically that viewers may become desensitized to violence and that the violent scenes may be perceived in a more positive light when juxtaposed with the more pleasant sexual scenes. Clips of scenes from slasher films were interspersed throughout the filmed message to assist subjects in understanding the effects. Subjects exposed to the pre-film message were somewhat less susceptible to the effects of the slasher films on the first day of the study than were those who had not been exposed to the message. Specifically, subjects in the pre-film message condition classified more scenes as instances of violence toward women than did subjects in the no-message condition. Subjects exposed to the pre-film message also found the film to be significantly more degrading to women, and the violence to be less realistic, than did subjects who did not receive the warning. These effects did not last beyond the first day of viewing, however.

Intons-Peterson and her colleagues developed pre-film briefings designed to be more long lasting. These briefings covered a wide range of information about rape and sexual violence toward women. College-age men then watched these messages so researchers could determine whether the negative effects of exposure to sexual violence could be countered by exposure to this information (Intons-Peterson & Roskos-Ewoldsen, 1989; Intons-Peterson et al., 1989). The rape pre-film briefing contained current information about rape drawn from Uniform Crime Statistics, described common effects of rape upon victims, and debunked some popular myths about rape by citing relevant statistics. The rape education group was more likely to think that the accused rapist in the videotape trial had caused injury to the victim than was the nonbriefed group. The briefing group's rejection of rape myths carried over to a delayed session two weeks after subjects had completed the experiment, whereas the nonbriefed group did not show extended effects.

Linz et al. (1990) tested the effectiveness of an intervention designed to modify reactions to eroticized violence in films, to decrease rape myth acceptance, and to sensitize viewers to the plight of a rape victim presented in a videotaped legal trial (Linz, Arluk, & Donnerstein, 1990). Male college students were brought into the laboratory and shown a documentary on the potentially negative psychological impact of sexually violent films on viewers and society and the two rape education films developed by Intons-Peterson et al. Later, the men viewed a violent erotic film and a videotaped sexual assault trial. The results indicated that levels of rape myth acceptance were lower for those men who had participated in the intervention groups. Men in these groups also indicated they were more depressed after viewing the erotic violent film, were more sympathetic to the victim portrayed in the rape trial, and were more likely to perceive the victim as not responsible for her own rape, than were subjects in the nonintervention conditions.

4. Pornography and Harms to Women: The Feminist Theory and Empirical Research

The feminist[1] perspective emphasizes that pornography depicts women as whores or prostitutes, and thus as receptacles for any sexual indignity and even rape and torture. In pornography, according to this perspective, women are dehumanized by being presented as sexual objects; in postures of sexual submission or in scenarios of degradation; as enjoying pain or humiliation or experiencing sexual pleasure at being raped; or in scenarios of injury and torture in a context that makes these conditions sexual. This normative theory assumes that pornography is a powerful socializing agent. Through pornography men are able to force on women their notions of what appropriate sexual relations between men and women are and can shape how women perceive themselves. Thus, pornography may be thought of as the graphic, sexually explicit subordination of women. Feminist theory asserts that pornography promotes sexual abuse of individual women and the social subordination of women as a class.

Such feminists are critical of both the moralist and the liberal free speech social perspectives. In their view, conservative-moral concerns with prurient appeal (sexual arousal) and offensiveness are misplaced. When sexual arousal is emphasized by feminists, it is not sexual arousal due to public displays of consenting sex, but arousal in response to women as objects of dominance, violence, and rape. Liberal concerns for freedom of speech ignore the fact that many forms of speech are controlled by the most powerful members of society—usually men rather than women. The liberal notion that all forms of speech should be unregulated is rejected because it does not recognize that the power men have over women to define them in pornography, has, in essence, silenced women.

The feminist approach, unlike the liberal approach, focuses on the effects pornography has on attitudes about women that may promote sexually abusive and discriminatory behaviors, rather than limiting its concerns to direct, specific physical harms. Rather than erring on the side of protecting individual liberties by limiting ourselves to the consideration of physical harms only, this position risks erring on the side of protecting women by taking into account the effects of pornography on attitudes and beliefs that may facilitate physical violence against women.

Research testing feminist socio-legal theory has examined pornography's effect on attitudes that justify violence toward women, undermine viewer sensitivity to female victims of rape and violence, and increase discriminatory and sexually aggressive behavior. Such behavior has been measured both indirectly in the laboratory and directly through self-reports of actual sexual aggression.

Whereas researchers guided by the liberal approach view words and pictures as harmful only if they directly effect aggressive behavior, particularly criminal activity, investigators influenced by feminists seek out more subtle (and possibly more widespread) effects, such as the endorsement of limiting roles for women, belief in myths about rape, and desensitization to violence against women. In their willingness to investigate attitudes and indirect indications of discrimination and aggression, these investigators have shunned a liberal First Amendment logic that limits harm to the *John hit Mary* sense (MacKinnon, 1984).

Researchers have also evaluated the notion that what is exciting about pornography for many men is the sexualization of subordination and violence. This research has focused on "normal" men and their inclinations toward aggression rather than focusing primarily on criminal or clinical groups.

Although research of this type has also considered individual differences, the variables that interest feminist researchers are not the same for those researchers adhering to the liberal position (such as sexual repression). Instead, just as feminists are most concerned about individuals who exhibit misogyny, the individual differences examined by social scientists influenced by feminists have been variables such as degree of attraction to sexual aggression, hostility toward women, and attitudes about rape.

Researchers influenced by feminism have empirically assessed whether these variables moderate the effects of exposure to pornography and other media, with particular focus on the possibility that the media contributes to a cultural climate that is more accepting of violence against women. The research therefore has not only studied the effects of materials that traditional obscenity law considers immoral, but has paid at least as much attention to materials that are not sexually explicit but portray violence against women or female subservience in a mildly sexualized context.

This perspective has also fostered research on the impact of pornography's message on women viewers themselves. Here, researchers have tested the impact of several types of pornographic depictions on female self-esteem, feelings of degradation, physiological, and emotional reactions following exposure. This research tests the feminist notion that pornography forces on women a male view of appropriate sexual relations between men and women and often shapes how women perceive themselves.

The Sexualization of Subordination and Violence

An example of a research topic derived from the feminist approach is the impact of *positive* versus *negative* outcome of rape in pornographic portrayals. Feminists contend that media portrayals of women deriving pleasure from being assaulted by men contribute to an ideology that justifies women's subordination and abuse (Brownmiller, 1975). To study this problem, investigators have devised experiments in which viewers are shown several versions of a rape in which all features are held constant except whether the victim was portrayed as involuntarily sexually aroused (*positive* outcome) or as reacting with disgust to the assault (*negative* outcome). Studies have compared the effects of such depictions on sexual arousal, attitudes, and aggressive behavior.

Sexual arousal to rape.   Two types of studies focus on the effects of positive and negative outcome manipulations on sexual arousal. The first examines whether these manipulations alter the degree of sexual arousal stimulated by the depictions themselves. The second examines whether exposure to different types of rape portrayals affects sexual arousal (and other reactions) to additional depictions presented later (a conditioning effect).

Findings of the first type are illustrated by Malamuth and Check (1983). In a preliminary session, men completed questionnaires about their sexual attitudes and behaviors. This included an item assessing attraction to sexual aggression (Malamuth, 1985a,1985b) by inquiring about the likelihood that the subject himself would rape if he could be assured of not being caught and punished (LR). On the basis of this item, subjects were classified as low or high LR. Several days later, the men listened to one of eight audiotapes of an interaction involving sexual intercourse between a man and a woman. The content of these depictions was systematically manipulated along the dimensions of consent (woman's consent versus nonconsent), pain (woman's pain versus no pain), and outcome (woman's arousal versus disgust).

Results for both self-reports and genital measures of sexual arousal indicated that when the woman was portrayed as experiencing disgust, both low and high LR subjects were less aroused sexually by the nonconsenting than they were by consenting depictions. However, when the woman was perceived as becoming aroused sexually, a very different pattern emerged: Low LR subjects were equally aroused to the consenting and the nonconsenting depictions, whereas high LR subjects showed greater arousal to the nonconsenting scenes. That is, there was a telling interaction between individual differences and variations in the content. Males who are likely to commit rape are particularly aroused when they see sexual aggression depicted without the woman's consent.

These data suggest that sexual violence may stimulate sexual arousal among some segments of the population. A sizable minority of the population (i.e., high LR subjects) may be more aroused by a rape depiction portraying victim arousal than by a consenting portrayal. More recent data (Heilbrun & Seis, 1988) also suggest that sexual violence may be a stimulant for a considerable proportion of the general male population.

What is the etiology of such arousal? A feminist approach emphasizes cultural attitudes, roles, and beliefs that justify sexual coercion. According to this view, men are socialized to believe that some degree of coercive sexuality is the norm, part of a *macho* dominant role for men. Women are socialized to accept a subservient role. Rape is an extreme point along a continuum of forced sexuality rather than a discrete, deviant act committed by only a few mentally ill men. Similarly, sexual arousal in response to aggression against unconsenting women, even among men who may never actually rape, can be seen as falling along such a continuum.

On the basis of such a theory, sexual arousal from aggression toward women ought to be associated with a set of beliefs that naturalize and justify male dominance and female submissiveness. An individual holding such beliefs views male-female relationships as fundamentally adversarial. Some of his attitudes could even be described as *rape suppor-tive*. To the extent that arousal from aggression reflects a hypermasculine macho orientation, it might be associated with a broader acceptance of aggression in nonsexual situations (Sanday, 1981). And, on the basis of the feminist approach, sexual arousal from aggression would not be an isolated response but one related to other inclinations toward violence against women.

There is research to support portions of this hypothesis. Malamuth and Check (1983) found that subjects who were more sexually aroused by aggression against women were more accepting of an ideology that justifies male aggression against and dominance over women and were somewhat more accepting of aggression in nonsexual situations as well. These subjects also reported more attraction to sexually coercive acts and were more likely to say that they would personally engage in such acts. The data appear to support feminist theoretical approaches that implicate cultural attitudes and roles as contributing to sexual arousal patterns and to coercive behavior.

Some research on adults has examined whether exposure to the fusion of sexual and aggressive images in media produces sustained changes in what "turns people on" sexually, but it has not shown such effects (e.g., Ceniti & Malamuth, 1984). This does not rule out a causal effect for exposure to pornography with youth, however, because sexual arousal patterns appear to be well established before adulthood (Abel, 1989).

Changes in perceptions and attitudes toward rape victims. Malamuth and his colleagues have conducted a series of studies examining the effects of exposure to sexual violence in the media on perceptions of rape and its victims. These studies have generally taken the following form: Male subjects were either exposed to depictions of mutually consenting sex, or rape in which the female victim eventually became aroused, or rape that was abhorred by the victim. Afterwards, the subjects were shown a rape depiction and asked about their perceptions of the act and the victim. Males exposed to the *positive* rape portrayal perceived the second rape as less negative (Malamuth & Check, 1980, 1980a, 1980b; Malamuth, Haber, & Feshbach, 1980) and more normal (Malamuth & Check, 1980a) than those first exposed to the other depictions. In addition, some research has asked male subjects how they think women in general would react to being victimized by sexual violence (Malamuth & Check, 1985). Those first exposed to a *positive* rape portrayal believed that a higher percentage of women would derive pleasure from being sexually assaulted. The effect of the portrayal was particularly apparent in men with self-reported inclinations to aggress against women.

Laboratory studies on aggressive behavior against women. A series of studies by Donnerstein examined effects of pornography on aggression against women (see Donnerstein, 1984, for a review). Donnerstein and Berkowitz (1981) studied male reactions to the female rape victim in the film. A common theme in violent pornography is that women are shown to derive pleasure from sexual aggression. Viewing an act of aggression in which the victim responds in a positive manner might well reduce aggressive inhibitions and justify aggression. In two experiments by Donnerstein and Berkowitz, male subjects were first angered by a male or female confederate. They were then shown one of four 5 minute film clips. One film was neutral and did not depict sex or violence. A second film was sexually explicit but did not contain any scenes of violence. The third and fourth films showed violent pornography. They depicted a young woman who comes to study with two men. Both have been drinking, and when the young woman sits between them she is shoved and forced to drink. She is then tied up, stripped, slapped, and raped by both men. In the positive ending version of the film, the woman is shown smiling at the end and in no way resisting. A narrative added to the film indicates that she eventually became a willing participant. In the negative film ending, the reactions of the woman are ambiguous, but the narrative indicates that she found the experience humiliating and disgusting. After viewing these films, all subjects were asked to rate them on several dimensions including aggressiveness and the degree to which the female in the film appeared to suffer.

Subjects' perceptions of the two rape films differed depending on the victim's reaction at the end of the film. It is important to remember that both films depicted the same acts of aggression; only the endings differed. Yet subjects who were exposed to the positive ending film saw it as less aggressive than those shown the negative ending. Furthermore, the woman in the positive ending film was seen as suffering less, enjoying herself more, and was considered more responsible for the aggerssion of the males.

What were the effects on aggression toward the women in the experiment? When subjects were angered by a male, there were no effects from exposure to any of the films. However, males exposed to either the negative or positive outcome violent pornography films increased their aggression toward the female who angered them. There were no increases in aggression among men exposed to the sexually explicit but nonviolent film.

These results suggest that (in a laboratory situation), violent pornography can increase aggression against women. While both types of violent pornography increased aggression equally, they likely did so for different reasons. The positive ending film may have suggested that aggression was acceptable. This is similar to the Malamuth (1978) study demonstrating that when subjects are given information that aggression is appropriate, exposure to violent pornography increases aggression toward a woman. It appears that a similar process was at work in the

Donnerstein and Berkowitz (1981) study. The negative-ending film may have had its influence because the pain and suffering of the woman in the film acted as a reinforcement for later aggression by males who were already predisposed to aggress.

Pornography and Discrimination Against Women

According to the feminist normative theory, pornography has other detrimental effects aside from increasing sexual violence. Feminists have implicated pornography in promoting bigotry and contempt for women and associated it with diminished opportunities for equality in employment, education, property, public accommodations, and public services. Interestingly, the courts, while finding the Indianapolis antipornography ordinance unconstitutional, did not disagree with the premise of the legislation that pornography produces and maintains the inferior social status of women. In fact, the Seventh Circuit Court proclaimed: "Depictions of subordination tend to perpetuate subordination. The subordinate status of women leads to affront and lower pay at work..." (*American Booksellers Association v. Hudnut*, appeal, 1986, p. 329).

Baron (1990) examined the idea that pornography contributes to sexual discrimination in a correlational study using pornographic magazine circulation rates and several indices of inequality of the sexes. Specifically, he tested this hypothesis: The higher the circulation rate of pornographic magazines the lower the level of gender equality. He constructed an index composed of 24 indicators of status of women relative to men in politics, economics, and legal rights. In the political sector, for example, he measured the percentage of state senate and house members and the percentage of mayors who were women. In the economic sector he counted the percent of women who were managers and administrators, and the percent of small business loans given to women. In the legal sector he noted whether or not the state had passed a fair employment practices act, equal pay laws, and statutes that define the physical abuse of a family member as a criminal offense. The measure of the prevalence of pornography was the same as that used in previous studies discussed in the previous chapter. In addition, several control variables, including a violence index, measures of acceptance of violence in each state, and the number of Southern Baptists in the state, were included in the analyses. The latter variable was included, according to the author, because many followers of that faith believe in the divine necessity of patriarchical authority and the natural inferiority of women (Falwell, 1980).

Baron's results showed exactly the opposite of what would be predicted by feminists. There was a strong positive correlation ($r = .56$) between circulation rates of pornographic magazines and gender equality in a state. But that was not the strongest predictor of scores on the gender equality index. The highest correlation was found between the presence of Southern Baptists in a state and that state's gender equality index. The more Southern Baptists in the state the lower the gender equality.

Baron (1990) was careful not to conclude that pornography consumption *causes* greater gender equality. Instead, he maintains that a third variable—political tolerance—may account for the abundance of pornography that is coupled with greater gender equality. In politically tolerant states there is both greater protection of free speech rights, including a lenient attitude toward objectionable speech such as pornography, and greater support for equality between men and women.

A Cultural Climate of Aggression Against Women

One important caveat to the study of pornography arising from the feminist approach to research is the recognition that media violence against women is not solely a matter of pornography. The crucial element for researchers is not the degree of sexual explicitness per se, as in the conservative-moral approach, but the broader messages conveyed in the material. Consequently, researchers operating in this perspective have not strictly relied on the use of materials that traditional obscenity law recognizes as sexually explicit, sexually arousing, or immoral. Content analyses reveal that many films that are not X-rated and not considered obscene portray as much sexual violence, and more nonsexual violence, than X-rated films (Yang & Linz, 1990).

Malamuth and Check (1981) found that mass media depictions that are not sexually explicit may also increase acceptance of violence against women. Male and female participants in two experimental conditions were given free tickets to view feature length films (on two different evenings) that included portrayals of women as victims of aggression. These films suggested either that the aggression was justified or that it had *positive* consequences. Subjects in the control condition were given tickets to other films (on the same evenings) that did not contain any sexual violence. The movies in both exposure conditions had been shown, with some editing, on national television. Subjects viewed these films with moviegoers who purchased tickets and were not part of the research. Classmates of the recruited subjects who did not see either of the films were also studied.

Several days after the films were viewed, a survey was administered to the entire class. The students were asked how much they accepted sexual aggression and wife battering, rape myths such as the belief that women secretly desire to be raped, and the view that sexual relations between men and women are adversarial (e.g., that women are sly and manipulating when out to attract a man). The students were not aware of the relationship between this survey—purportedly administered by a polling agency—and the earlier movies some of them had seen as part of an ostensibly unrelated study. Exposure to the experimental films portraying *positive* effects significantly increased male (but not female) acceptance of sexual aggression and wife battering. A similar pattern was observed for rape myth acceptance. Taken together, the data illustrate the detrimental effects of media messages, even when they do not appear in a sexually explicit context, on men's attitudes about violence against women.

Research focusing on widely available slasher films is also relevant to the feminist claim that media other than the highly sexually explicit kind can nevertheless harm women (Linz, Donnerstein, & Adams, 1989; Linz, Donnerstein, & Penrod, 1984; Linz et al., 1988). In these films rape is not often portrayed, but scenes of extreme violence are juxtaposed with mildly sexually arousing scenes. According to film critic Janet Maslin, in a slasher film

> the carnage is usually preceded by some sort of erotic prelude: footage of pretty young bodies in the shower, or teens changing into nighties for the slumber party, or anything that otherwise lulls the audience into a mildly sensual mood . . . The speed and ease with which one's feelings can be transformed from sensuality into viciousness may surprise even those quite conversant with the links between sexual and violent urges. (Maslin, 1982, p. 2)

In a study by Linz, Donnerstein, and Penrod (1988), college men were exposed to nearly eight hours of unedited, feature length films. Experimental subjects viewed one of three types of films: slasher films, nonviolent (teenage sex) comedies, or sexually explicit nonviolent movies. Or, they participated in the study as *no exposure* control subjects. After subjects had completed their final film viewing session, they reported their empathy for rape victims in general (Dietz, Blackwell, Daley,& Bently, 1982) and watched a videotaped, condensed reenactment of a complete rape trial. After viewing the trial, they completed scales designed to measure sympathy for the victim in the trial. The men exposed to slasher films, when compared with the other film conditions, showed less sympathy for the alleged rape victim and lower levels of rape empathy.

The Combination of Sexually Explicit Media With Other Variables

Researchers have been interested in whether exposure to pornography affects behavior mostly through *indirect* effects (e.g., Malamuth, 1986, 1989b). By this term, researchers mean effects mediated by other variables (Kenny & Judd, 1986).

An example of this type of mediated effect was found by McKenzie-Mohr and Zanna (1990). Their study demonstrated that exposure to pornography can prime men to view women as sexual objects, but this effect does not manifest itself in all men. Rather, those men classified as *sex-typical* (as measured by the Sex Role Inventory; Bem, 1984) having *gender-schemas* about men and women that emphasize traditional sex roles, are more likely to be influenced by pornography than are men classified as *androgynous* or less likely to rely on sex-typical schemas for processing social information. McKenzie-Mohr and Zanna first classified men whose views were considered sex-typical and then showed them pornography. Afterwards, the men were asked to participate in an interview with a female confederate of the experimenter. Men who were classified as sex-typical and who viewed pornography were judged to be more sexually motivated toward the interviewer, stood closer to the female confederate during the interview, and recalled more information about the interviewer's physical appearance and less of what she said, compared to androgynous men and to sex-typical men who had not viewed pornography.

In speculation about more complicated mediated effects, Malamuth (1986) suggests that sexually violent media may affect men's attitudes, which, if combined with several other factors, may in turn, affect aggressive behavior in naturalistic settings. This is not to say that the mass media are the most or even one of the most powerful influences on sexually violent behavior. Rather, media may be only one of many fac- tors that interact to effect responses. The nature of the effect and the degree of influence of sexually violent media may depend on, among other things, the psychological background of the person exposed to the media stimuli, and the sociocultural context in which exposure takes place (Malamuth, 1989b).

Malamuth (1986) breaks down the variables thought to set the stage for sexual aggression into three classes: motivation, disinhibition, and opportunity. Motivation for sexual aggression includes sexual arousal to aggression, hostility toward women, and dominance as a motive for sex. Disinhibition to commit sexual aggression includes attitudes condoning aggression and antisocial personality characteristics. Opportunity to aggress sexually is indicated by the personal sexual experience. These aggression predictors were each somewhat related to self-reports of sexual aggression, but *combinations* of these variables produced far more accurate predictions of sexual aggression. Men who had high scores on all of the predictor variables tended to be highly aggressive sexually. That is, these factors tend to reinforce one another.

The Effects of Pornography on Female Viewers

Research has tested the feminist contention that pornography endorses men's view of appropriate sexual relations between men and women and shapes how women perceive themselves. Systematic content analyses of pornographic and nonpornographic violent movies (slasher films) has identified themes that are potentially degrading to women. In one study, videocassettes were randomly drawn from lists of adult movie titles and the content was analyzed for themes of dominance and exploitation (Cowan, Lee, Levy, & Snyder, 1988). The researchers looked for *dominant scenes*, in which one participant is controlling the sex act, and *status inequality*, in which one participant is subordinate; indicators of status inequality include age differences, wealth disparities, clothing, occupation, and race. Most of the dominance involved men over women—of 124 scenes characterized by dominance, 78% were dominated by men. Cowan and O'Brien (1990) examined the contents of more than 50 slasher films (containing more than 470 victims). They focused on violence directed toward and committed by women versus men, how often victims survived their attacks, and the juxtaposition of sex and violence. They found that the slashers in these films were primarily men and that often sexiness was paired with the death of female victims.

The impact of degrading and unequal power depictions on female viewers has been studied in several ways. Cowan (1990) examined college women's reactions to pornographic films. Film content was coded for themes of dominance and status inequality as in Cowan et al. (1988), for themes such as *objectification* (sexual activity that treats the female as an object or plaything), *availability* (showing that the female is available to anyone who wants her and is undiscriminating in her choice of partners), *penis/semen worship* (scenes revolving around worship of the penis and the idea that to ejaculate is central to female's satisfaction), and *sexually explicit behavior* (activity that is explicit and mutual but does not indicate an affectionate personal relationship between people). Cowan then asked an independent group of female subjects to react to these scenes. She found that female viewers felt most degraded, and were most disgusted, by scenes that portrayed *objectification, dominance,* and *penis worship*. They felt least disgusted and degraded by explicit sex scenes.

Krafka, Penrod, Donnerstein, and Linz (1992) examined women's attitudes toward female victims in other contexts after they were exposed to (a) sexually explicit but nonviolent stimuli, (b) sexually explicit stimuli, (c) sexually violent stimuli, or (d) graphically violent but not sexually explicit stimuli (slasher films). After one week's viewing of one of these film types the women were asked to serve as mock jurors in a simulated rape trial. Both types of violent stimuli (but *not* the sexually explicit nonviolent stimuli) produced depression on the first day of viewing. This effect diminished across time and the violent films were rated as less degrading to women by the fourth day (both measures indicate a desensitization effect). Interestingly, the women who saw the violent films were, like men in the studies on slasher films described above, *less* sensitive toward the victim in the rape trial than were those who saw other types of films. This is an indication that women, like men, become desensitized to violence against women as a function of exposure to sexual violence in the media.

Note

1. We consider the *feminist* perspective as an *archtype* in our discussion. We realize that there are many individuals who object to the MacKinnon/Dworkin position on pornography. Many feminists embrace liberal philosophies concerning freedom of speech while still maintaining that women are harmed by pornography.

5. The Contributions of Each Approach to Scientific Research and Social Policy

The conservative-moralist, feminist, and liberal perspectives are normative theories that guide expectations about what effects sexually explicit communications will have on the individual and society. These theories stem from conceptual definitions that focus on different aspects of sexually explicit communication. The conservative-moralist focuses on the *obscene*: that which is offensive, disgusting, shameful, and contrary to an accepted standard for sexual behavior. The feminist perspective views many sexual depictions as *pornography*: literally, descriptions of acts of prostitutes, or the portrayal of women as such. The liberal holds that many sexually explicit depictions are *erotic*, referring to sexual expression between consenting adults.

As a normative theory, the obscenity perspective focuses on the effect of sexual arousal in the individual reader or viewer, to practices that are disgusting and offensive. It suggests that many sexually explicit materials are an attack on basic societal and religious values, and that the readers and viewers may become desensitized to immoral acts in general. The feminist interpretation assumes harm to all women in portraying a woman as happy in sexual enslavement and as existing merely for the pleasure of men, and harm to particular women, presumably when certain men internalize this message and act upon it. In contrast to both, the erotica perspective suggests that sexually explicit materials lead to harmless fantasy, providing stimulation in some persons' sex lives; erotica may even be sexually liberating for the reader or viewer.

These normative theories have been the springboard for communication researchers to derive testable hypotheses. Researchers have asked: What are the consequences of exposure to sexually explicit material if the viewer is exposed to depictions that sexually arouse but offend and disgust or exceed moral limits, or to those where women depicted as prostitutes and sex objects, or to depictions perceived as erotic and pleasurable sexual fantasy? In the preceding chapters we have surveyed some of the answers to these questions provided by researchers who have deliberately (or inadvertently) adopted one of the three perspectives.

Unique Contributions of Each Approach

Early research by the liberal 1970 commission (e.g., Ben-Veniste, 1970; Kutchinsky, 1970) formulated questions about pornography's effects in narrow behavioral terms. They asked questions such as: Does pornography increase violent crime? To date, we have discovered that it probably does not, at least under the conditions studied. If left to the liberal perspective, the question of pornography's effects would appear to be settled. In fact, those liberal policy makers recommended relinquishing all controls on sexually explicit material in 1970.

Questions raised from both the conservative-moralist and the feminist perspectives have continued to motivate research surprisingly relevant to liberal normative theory. As we noted in the last chapter, for example, Baron (1990) examined the relationship between pornography magazine circulation and behavioral indications of the status of women relative to men in politics, economics, and legal status in the United States. Contrary to what might have been expected from the feminist theory, he found a *positive* relationship between the presence of pornography in a state and greater civil rights for women. Baron suggests, consistent with the liberal approach, that in politically tolerant states there is greater protection of free speech rights, a more lenient attitude toward objectionable speech such as pornography, and greater support for equality between men and women.

From the liberal perspective, laboratory studies finding greater aggression against women, or finding attitudes facilitative of self-reported violence against women following exposure to pornography, are not sufficiently connected to more serious antisocial behaviors to justify repression of speech. This perspective does not disallow the possibility that broader, less tangible effects than changes in rape rates and other social statistics might exist, however. Research on the effects of *more speech* or corrective speech to rectify the negative effects suggested by laboratory studies of exposure to pornography, is perfectly consistent with a liberal theory of effects. In this vein, researchers have concentrated on development and testing of educational programs designed to counter the ideas presented in pornography—an attempt to further open up the marketplace of ideas.

The liberal orientation also has the capacity to generate new research. As we noted above, once liberal researchers had concluded that one of the most pervasive effects of exposure to pornography was a benign form of boredom, they turned their attention to the study of conservative-moralists who disapproved of sexually explicit materials in hope of understanding those critics' negative reactions. Further focus on individual differences can help us understand public and private tolerance for sexually explicit depictions and can also help identify a variety of other moderators of reactions to such materials (e.g., sexual arousal, long term consumption, use as a fantasy stimulant).

Questions about habituation to pornography (that originally excited one sexually), or about feelings of disgust and offensiveness, might never have been addressed if not for the perspective brought by the moral conservative (e.g., Zillmann, Bryant, Comisky, & Medoff, 1981; Zillmann & Sapolsky, 1977). Researchers operating from liberal assumptions would not have considered the potential repercussions of such diminished sexual arousal on attraction to more extreme (more sexually explicit or more graphically violent) images (e.g., Zillmann & Bryant, 1982, 1986). Liberals also might not have seriously considered the effects of pornography on attitudes toward promiscuity at the expense of monogamy, or on the value placed on marriage or having children (e.g., Zillmann & Bryant, 1988).

Neither the liberal nor the moralist would have asked about the possibility that pornography might foster an attitude of harmful discrimination against women, which has been the focus of researchers guided by the feminist perspective. Nor would they have been concerned (as have feminist researchers) about comparisons with nonpornographic materials that might be equally likely to foster violence against women.

Research from a feminist approach has also led to systematic assessment of more subtle attitudinal effects that form the basis of discrimination and cognitive sexism. The approach has attempted to assess the place of mass media depictions in a broader culture of acceptance of violence and discrimination against women. This has contributed to a more thorough investigation of the role of the media within the context of other societal and individual variables. This multifaceted approach suggests a longitudinal investigation of both cultural and individual difference factors that may explain much sexual violence (e.g., Malamuth, 1986; Malamuth, Heavey, & Linz, in press).

Overlap Among the Approaches

Among communication scientists there are several generally accepted criteria for evaluating communication theory (see Chaffee & Berger, 1987). Two of the most important are: the ability of the theory to support the available data and the fruitfulness of the theory for generating new research. We suggest that the conservative-moralist, liberal, and feminist approaches have all been of considerable value regarding the second of these two criteria. However, the ability of one theory to account for the data better than the others is questionable. We cannot, at this stage, clearly prefer one theory over another. Each predicts unique effects (or is convinced of the lack of other effects) for exposure to sexually explicit material, and each has found some support for its predictions. There have been no systematic attempts to pit these theories directly against each other. This would require determining the conditions under which they make competing predictions so that they can be empirically compared. So far, no one has specified these conditions.

We have emphasized the incompatibilities among the approaches in this book in order to illustrate what each perspective brings to the study of pornography. Now, it may be desirable to integrate aspects of these theories within a larger metatheory. Perhaps it is time to search for explanations of effects that underlie all three approaches. We have not thought of a unifying theory, nor are we convinced that any such theory is possible. Integration of the perspectives must overcome the divisiveness inherent in the origin of these concepts—the policy arena.

Returning the Concepts to Their Origins

The scientific questions concerning pornography effects are inseparable from the social policy context in which they arose. Many of the scientific issues discussed in this book might never have been raised if they did not have a bearing on policy. Researchers' interpretations of findings derived from the conservative-moral, liberal, and feminist normative approaches often imply that one social policy alternative should be favored over another. It is important to recognize the subtle ways in which science and policy are connected in this research area.

Communication scientists operating from each perspective have criticized the research findings of those in opposing theoretical camps. These debates nearly always appear to be about the types of evidence that would qualify as support for the conclusion that pornography produces a significant harm; or, what threshold of harm, objectively or scientifically speaking, must be reached before any action should be taken to limit pornographic depictions or access to them. These disagreements however, are not merely about methodology. The methods employed by research practitioners within each perspective and the judgments about whether or not an important effect has been found are influenced by what scientists think *ought* to be done about the societal problem of pornography.

In Chapter 3 we noted that some researchers (e.g., Brannigan & Goldenberg, 1987) are critical of relationships discovered in the laboratory (see also Fisher & Barak, 1991). They feel that the laboratory situation is so far removed from the circumstances about which we "legitimately are worried" and the results are "so qualified in terms of their equivalence to existing social circumstances" that they are almost useless. To these scientists, legislation based on these experimental findings is unwarranted. To them, results from laboratory studies that measure analogs to aggressive behavior, or findings involving negative changes in attitudes toward women, fall below the threshold necessary for establishing a harm effect. These authors seem to believe that the determination of a threshold for an acceptable result is purely an objective matter of scientific methodology.

We hope have shown in this book that outcome measures such as crime rates or physical harm are chosen for reasons other than the dictates of proper methodology alone. Direct physical harm is the preferred dependent measure for researchers who feel it is important to err on the side of protecting individual liberties. Critiques such as Brannigan and Goldenberg's (1987) are as much statements of what *ought* to be done about the problem of pornography in society as they are discussions about acceptable scientific methodology. Research guided by the feminist perspective, as we have noted in Chapter 4, may focus on other dependent measures such as attitudes that are merely *facilita-*

tive of violence or discrimination, rather than on direct violence as an important outcome variable. These effects are chosen because the scientist believes that one ought to err on the side of defending women's rights. Feminists take into account the effects that aggressive pornography or slasher films have on attitudes and beliefs that may facilitate physical violence against women, make people more tolerant of violence against women, or foster a climate of legitimation for violence against women.

We do not wish to be misunderstood. We believe that the scientists offering a critique of their peers are honestly attempting to evaluate the quality of the evidence. These critiques can offer valuable insights into design flaws in the research. There are problems, however, when a critique is offered as if it were simply "objective science."

"Objective" evaluations could continue endlessly because of the enduring nature of the ideologies guiding researchers' choices of methodologies and evaluations of the data. Social scientists who have reviewed the research from a liberal perspective (e.g., Brannigan & Goldenberg, 1987) conclude that the scientific evidence does not merit any harm conclusion. Adopting a feminist perspective, one could just as easily conclude that the evidence strongly supports harm to women and to society at large (e.g., Russell, 1988). Reviews of the evidence are guided by the powerful influence of the underlying philosophical assumptions and social values we have discussed in this book. Whether or not any of the scientists involved in research from the point of view of one of the three perspectives would reject their basic premises in the face of contrary data gathered from another perspective is questionable.

What is clear is that the findings from scientific investigations have been used by conservative-moral, liberal, and feminist policymakers to support their positions on what is to be done about the problem of pornography. Policymakers, taking one or another of the positions, have tended to ignore potentially conflicting evidence from competing points of view. We suspect that this will always be the case. Policymakers will always use scientific findings to bolster their own normative positions. As discoverers of these findings, we should seek to recognize the biases of particular groups and be appropriately cautious about generalizing from our data depending on the group and its goals. (See Linz, Malamuth, & Beckett, 1992; and Linz, Penrod, & Donnerstein, 1986, for a more detailed account of the uses and misuses of pornography research and suggestions for dissemination of research findings to policy groups.) Finally, as discoverers of research facts about pornography, we should strive to recognize our own normative theory about effects. Once recognized, these assumptions can be more clearly stated. When each theoretical position is fully delineated, others may more clearly ask their questions from competing perspectives.

References

Abel, G. G., Barlow, D. H., Blanchard, E. B., & Guild, D. (1977). The components of rapists' sexual arousal. *Archives of General Psychiatry, 34,* 395-403; 895-903.

Abel, G. G., Becker, J. V., Mittelman, M., Cunningham-Rathner, J., Rouleau, J. L., & Murphy, W. D. (1987). Self-reported sex crimes of nonincarcerated paraphiliacs. *Journal of Interpersonal Violence, 2,* 3-25.

American Booksellers Association v. Hudnut. 598 F. Supp. 1316; aff'd. 771 F.2nd 323 (1986).

Attorney General's Commission on Pornography: Final Report. (1986, July). Washington, DC: Department of Justice.

Bandura, A. (1973). *Aggression: A social learning process.* New York: Prentice Hall.

Barbaree, H. E., Marshall, W. L., & Lanthier, R. D. (1979). Deviant sexual arousal in rapists. *Behavior Research and Therapy, 17,* 215-222.

Barnes v. Glen Theatre Inc. (1991).

Baron, L. (1990). Pornography and gender equality: An empirical analysis. *The Journal of Sex Research, 27*(3), 363-380.

Baron, L., & Straus, M. A. (1984). Sexual stratification, pornography, and rape in the United States. *Pornography and sexual aggression* (pp. 185-209). Orlando, FL: Academic Press.

Baron, R. (1974). Sexual arousal and physical aggression: The inhibiting influence of "cheesecake" and nudes. *Bulletin of the Psychonmic Society, 3,* 337-339.

Baron, R., & Bell, P. (1973). Sexual arousal and aggression by males: Effects of type of erotic stimuli and prior provocation. *Journal of Personality and Social Psychology, 35,* 79-87.

Baxter, D. J., Marshall, W. L., Barbaree, H. E., Davidson, P. R., & Malcolm, P. B. (1984). Deviant sexual behavior differentiating sex offenders by criminal and personal history, psychometric measures, and sexual response. *Criminal Justice Behavior, 11,* 477-501.

Bem, S. L. (1984). The measurement of psychological androgeny. *Journal of Consulting and Clinical Psychology, 42,* 155-162.

Ben-Veniste, R. (1970). Pornography and sex crime—The Danish experience. *Technical reports of the Presidential Commission on Obscenity and Pornography* (Vol. 7). Washington, DC: Government Printing Office.

Brandenburg v. Ohio, 395 U.S. 444 (1969).

Brannigan, A. (1986, March). Crimes from comics: Social and political determinants of reform of the victoria obscenity law 1938-1954. *AUST & Nz Journal of Criminology, 19,* 23-42.

Brannigan, A., & Goldenberg, S. (1987). The study of aggressive pornography: The vicissitudes of relevance. *Critical Studies in Mass Communication, 4,* 262-283.

64

Brownmiller, S. (1975). *Against our will: Men, women and rape.* New York: Simon & Schuster.

Bryant, J. (1986). Testimony before the Attorney General's Commission on Pornography. Washington, DC.

Butler v. Queen (1992). Supreme Court of Canada.

Byrne, D. (1982). Predicting human sexual behavior. In A. G. Kraut (Ed.), *The G. Stanley Hall Lecture Series, Vol. 2* (pp. 207-254). Washington, DC: American Psychological Association.

Byrne, D., Fisher, J. D., Lamberth, J., & Mitchell, H. E. (1974). Evaluations of erotica: Facts or feelings? *Journal of Personality and Social Psychology, 29,* 111-116.

Byrne, D., & Kelley, K. (1981). *An introduction to personality* (3rd ed.). Englewood Cliffs, NJ: Prentice Hall.

Byrne, D., & Lamberth, J. (1970). The effect of erotic stimuli on sex arousal, evaluative responses, and subsequent behavior. *Technical reports of the Presidential Commission on Obscenity and Pornography* (Vol. 8). Washington, DC: Government Printing Office.

Ceniti, J., & Malamuth, N. (1984). Effects of repeated exposure to sexually violent or nonviolent stimuli on sexual arousal to rape and nonrape depictions. *Behaviour Research and Therapy, 22,* 535-548.

Chaffee, S., & Berger, C. (1987). What communication scientists do. In *The Handbook of Communication Research.* Newbury Park, CA: Sage.

Check, J.V.P., & Malamuth, N. M. (1984). Can there be positive effects of participation in pornography experiments? *Journal of Sex Research, 20,* 14-31.

Christensen, F. M. (1990). Cultural and ideological bias in pornography research. *Philosophy of the Social Sciences, 20*(3), 351-375.

Cleland, J. (1982). *Fanny Hill: Memoirs of a woman of pleasure.* New York: Dell.

Cook, R. F., & Fosen, R. H. (1970). Pornography and the sex offender: Patterns of exposure and immediate arousal effects of pornographic stimuli. *Technical reports of the Commission on Obscenity and Pornography* (Vol. 7). Washington, DC: Government Printing Office.

Cowan, G. (1990). *What is degrading in pornography? Through women's eyes.* Paper presented at the annual meeting of the Western Psychological Association, Los Angeles.

Cowan, G., Lee, C., Levy, D., & Snyder, D. (1988). Dominance and equality in X-rated videocassettes. *Psychology of Women Quarterly, 12,* 299-311.

Cowan, G., & O'Brien, M. (1990). *Gender survival versus death in slasher films: A content analysis.* Unpublished mauscript, California State University, San Bernardino.

Davis, K. E., & Braucht, G. N. (1970). Exposure to pornography, character, and sexual deviance. *Technical reports of the Presidential Commission on Obscenity and Pornography* (Vol. 7). Washington, DC: Government Printing Office.

Dietz, S., Blackwell, K., Daley, P., & Bently, B. (1982). Measurement of empathy toward rape victims and rapists. *Journal of Personality and Social Psychology, 43,* 372-384.

Donnerstein, E. (1984). Pornography: Its effect on violence against women. In N. M. Malamuth & E. Donnerstein (Eds.), *Pornography and sexual aggression.* Orlando, FL: Academic Press.

Donnerstein, E., & Berkowitz, L. (1981). Victim reactions in aggressive erotic films as a factor in violence against women. *Journal of Personality and Social Psychology, 41,* 710-724.

Donnerstein, E., & Wilson, D. W. (1976). Effects of noise and perceived control on ongoing and subsequent aggressive behavior. *Journal of Personality and Social Psychology, 34*, 774-781.

Downs, D. (1989). *The new politics of pornography.* Chicago: University of Chicago Press.

Dworkin, A. (1974). *Effect of pornography on women and children.* Testimony at the Hearings before the Subcommittee on Juvenile Justice of the Committee on the Judiciary, 98th Cong., 2nd Sess. 227-255.

Falwell, J. (1980). *Listen America.* Garden City, NY: Doubleday.

Fisher, W., & Barak, A. (1991). Pornography, erotica, and behavior: More questions than answers. *International Journal of Law and Psychiatry, 14*, 65-83.

Garcia, L. T., & Griffitt, W. (1978). Impact of testimonial evidence as a funciton of witness characteristics. *Bulletin of the Psychometric Society, 11*, 37-40.

Gardiner, H. C. (1967). Erotic literature. *New Catholic Encyclopedia Vol. 5.* New York: McGraw Hill.

Gerrard, M., & Gibbons, F. X. (1982). Sexual experience, sex guilt, and sexual moral reasoning. *Journal of Personality, 50*, 435-439.

Goldstein, M., Kant, H., Judd, L., Rice, C., & Geen, R. (1970). Exposure to pornography and sexual behavior in deviant and normal groups. *Technical reports of the Presidential Commission on Obscenity and Pornography* (Vol. 7). Washington, DC: Government Printing Office.

Gould, L. (1977). Pornography for women. In *Human Sexuality in Today's World.* Boston: Little-Brown.

Gray, S. H. (1982). Exposure to pornography and aggression toward women: The case of the angry male. *Social Problems, 29*, 387-398.

Grings, W. W., & Dawson, M. E. (1978). *Emotions and bodily responses: A psychophysiological approach.* New York: Academic Press.

Gross, L. (1983). Pornography and social science. *Journal of Communication, 33*, 107-111.

Gunther, A. (1991). *Origins of opinion on pornography restrictions.* Unpublished manuscript, University of Wisconsin-Madison.

Heilbrun, A. B., & Seis, D. (1988). Erotic value of female distress in sexually explicit photographs. *Journal of Sex Research, 24*, 47-57.

Howard, J. L., Reifler, C. B., & Liptzin, M. B. (1971). Effects of exposure to pornography. In *Technical reports of the Presidential Commission on Obscenity and Pornography* (Vol. 8; pp. 97-132). Washington, DC: Government Printing Office.

Intons-Peterson, M. J., Roskos-Ewoldsen, B. (1989). Mitigating the effects of violent pornography. In S. Gubar & J. Hoff-Wilson (Eds.), *For adult users, only.* Bloomington: Indiana University Press.

Intons-Peterson, M. J., Roskos-Ewoldsen, B., Thomas, L., Shirley, M., & Blut, D. (1989). Will educational materials reduce the negative effects of exposure to sexual violence? *Journal of Social and Clinical Psychology, 8*, 256-275.

Jacobellis v. Ohio, 378 U.S. 184 (1964).

Jarvie, I. C. (1986) Methodological and conceptual problems in the study of pornography and violence. In *Thinking about society: Theory and practice.* Dordrecht: Reidel.

Jarvie, I. C. (1987). The sociology of the pornography debate. *Philosophy of the Social Sciences, 17*, 257-275.

Johnson, W. T., Kupperstein, L. R., & Peters, J. J. (1970). Sex offenders' experience with erotica. In *Technical reports of the Presidential Commission on Obscenity and Pornography* (Vol. 7). Washington, DC: Government Printing Office.

66

Kelley, K. (1985a). Sexual attitudes as determinants of the motivational properties of exposure to erotica. *Personality and Individual Differences, 6*(3), 391-393.

Kelley, K. (1985b). The effects of sexual and/or aggressive film exposure on helping, hostility, and attitudes about the sexes. *Journal of Research in Personality, 19,* 472-483.

Kelley, K., & Byrne, D. (1983). Assessment of sexual responding: Arousal, affect, and behavior. In J. Cacioppo & R. Petty (Eds.), *Social psychophysiology: A sourcebook* (pp. 467-490). New York: Guilford Press.

Kenny, D. A., & Judd, C. M. (1984). Estimating nonlinear and interactive effects of latent variables. *Psychological Bulletin, 96,* 201-210.

Kingsley International Pictures Corp. v. New York. 360 U.S. 684, 689-690, 79 S. Ct. 1362, 1366 (1959).

Kogan, N. (1956). Authoritarianism and repression. *Journal of Abnormal and Social Psychology, 53,* 34-37.

Krafka, S., Penrod, S., Donnerstein, E., & Linz, D. (1992). Sexually explicit, sexually aggressive and violent media: The effect of naturalistic exposure on females. Unpublished manuscript, University of Wisconsin.

Kupperstein, L., & Wilson, W. C. (1970). Erotica and anti-social behavior: An analysis of selected social indicator statistics. In *Technical reports of the Presidential Commission on Obscenity and Pornography* (Vol. 7). Washington, DC: Government Printing Office.

Kutchinsky, B. (1970). Pornography in Denmark: Pieces of a jigsaw puzzle collected around New Year 1970. In *Technical reports of the Presidential Commission on Obscenity and Pornography* (Vol. 4). Washington, DC: Government Printing Office.

Kutchinsky, B. (1991). Pornography and rape: Theory and practice? Evidence from crime data in four countries where pornography is easily available. *International Journal of Law and Psychiatry, 14,* 147-164.

Lahey, K. A. (1991). Pornography and harm: Learning to listen to women. *International Journal of Law and Psychiatry, 14*(1/2), 117-132.

Lawrence, D. H. (1968). *Lady Chatterley's lover.* New York: Bantam.

Linz, D., Arluk, I., & Donnerstein, E. (1990). Mitigating the negative effects of sexually violent mass media through pre-exposure briefings. *Communication Research, 17*(5), 641-674.

Linz, D., Donnerstein, E., & Adams, S. (1989). Physiological desensitization and judgments about female victims of violence. *Human Communication Research, 15*(4), 509-522.

Linz, D., Donnerstein, E., Bross, M., & Chapin, M. (1986). Mitigating the influence of violence on television and sexual violence in the media. In R. Blanchard (Ed.), *Advances in the study of aggression* (Vol. 2; pp. 165-194). New York: Academic Press.

Linz, D., Donnerstein, E., Land, K., McCall, P., Scott, J., Klein, L. J., Shafer, B. J., & Lance, L. (1991, Spring). Estimating community tolerance for obscenity: The use of social science evidence. *Public Opinion Quarterly,* 80-112.

Linz, D., Donnerstein, E., & Penrod, S. (1984). The effects of multiple exposures to filmed violence against women. *Journal of Communication, 34,* 130-147.

Linz, D., Donnerstein, E., & Penrod, S. (1988). Long-term exposure to violent and sexually degrading depictions of women. *Journal of Personality and Social Psychology, 55*(5), 758-768.

Linz, D., Malamuth, N., & Beckett, C. (1992). Civil liberties and research on the effects of pornography. In P. Suedfeld & P. Tetlock (Eds.), *Psychology and social policy* (pp. 149-162). New York: Hemisphere.

Linz, D., Penrod, S., & Donnerstein, E. (1986). Media violence and antisocial behavior: Alternative legal policies. *Journal of Social Issues, 42* (3), 171-194.

Linz, D., Turner, C., Hesse, B., & Penrod, S. (1984). Bases of liability for injuries produced by media portrayals of violent pornography. In N. Malamuth & E. Donnerstein (Eds.), *Pornography and sexual aggression* (pp. 277-302). New York: Academic Press.

MacKinnon, C. (1984). Not a moral issue. *Yale Law and Policy Review, 2,* 321-345.

Malamuth, N. M. (1978). *Erotica, aggression, and perceived appropriateness.* Paper presented at 86th annual convention of the American Psychological Association, Toronto, Canada.

Malamuth, N. M. (1986). Predictors of naturalistic sexual aggression. *Journal of Personality and Social Psychology, 50*(5), 953-962.

Malamuth, N. M. (1989a, February). The attraction to sexual aggression scale: Part one. *The Journal of Sex Research, 25,* 26-49.

Malamuth, N. M. (1989b). Sexually violent media, thought patterns, and antisocial behavior. *Public Communication and Behavior, 2,* 159-204.

Malamuth, N. M., & Check, J.V.P. (1980a). Penile tumescence and perceptual responses to rape as a function of victim's perceived reactions. *Journal of Applied Social Psychology, 10,* 528-547.

Malamuth, N. M., & Check, J.V.P. (1980b). Sexual arousal to rape and consenting depictions: The importance of the woman's arousal. *Journal of Abnormal Psychology, 89,* 763-766.

Malamuth, N. M., & Check, J.V.P. (1981). The effects of mass media exposure on acceptance of violence against women: A field experiment. *Journal of Research in Personality, 15,* 436-446.

Malamuth, N. M., & Check, J.V.P. (1983). Sexual arousal to rape depictions: Individual differences. *Journal of Abnormal Psychology, 92*(1), 55-67.

Malamuth, N. M., & Check, J.V.P. (1984). Debriefing effectiveness following exposure to pornographic rape depictions. *Journal of Sex Research, 20,* 1-13.

Malamuth, N. M., & Check, J.V.P. (1985). The effects of aggressive pornography on beliefs of rape myths: Individual differences. *Journal of Research in Personality, 19,* 299-320.

Malamuth, N., Haber, S., & Feshbach, S. (1980). Testing hypotheses regarding rape: Exposure to sexual violence, sex differences, and the "normality" of rapists. *Journal of Research in Personality, 14,* 121-137.

Malamuth, N., Heavey, C. L., & Linz, D. (in press). Predicting men's aggression against women: Research contributing to the develoment of the confluence model of sexual aggression. In N. G. Hall & R. Hirschman (Eds.), *Sexual Aggression: Issues in etiology and assessment, treatment and policy.* New York: Hemisphere.

Mann, J., Sidman, J., & Starr, S. (1970). Effects of erotic films on sexual behavior of married couples. In *Technical reports of the Presidential Commission on Obscenity and Pornography* (Vol. 8). Washington, DC: Government Printing Office.

Marshall, W. L., & Barbaree, H. E. (1984). A behavioral view of rape. *International Journal of Law and Psychiatry, 7,* 51-77.

Maslin, J. (1982, November 11). Bloodbaths debase movies and audiences. *New York Times,* p. 2.

McKay, H. B., & Dolff, D. J. (1985). The impact of pornography: An analysis of research and summary of findings.*Working papers on pornography and prostitution, Report #13.* Ottawa: Department of Justice.

McKenzie-Mohr, D., & Zanna, M. P. (1990). Treating women as sexual objects: Look to the (gender schematic) male who has viewed pronography. *Personality and Social Psychology Bulletin, 16,* 296-308.

Memoirs v. Massachusetts 383 U.S. 413 (1966).

Michael, R. P., & Zumpe, D. (1978). Potency in male rhesus monkeys: Effects of continuously receptive females. *Science, 200,* 451-453.

Miller v. California, 413 U.S. 15 (1973).

Mosher, D. L. (1970). Sex callousness toward women. In *Technical reports of the Presidential Commission on Obscenity and Pornography: Erotica and antisocial behavior* (Vol. 7). Washington, DC: Government Printing Office.

Mosher, D. L. (1971). Psychological reactions to pornographic films. In *Technical reports of the Presidential Commission on Obscenity and Pornography* (Vol. 8). Washington DC: Government Printing Office.

Mosher, D. L. (1973). Sex differences, sex experience, sex guilt, and explicitly sexual films. *Journal of Social Issues, 29,* 95-112.

Mueller, C. W., & Donnerstein, E. (1977). The effects of humor-induced arousal upon aggressive behavior. *Journal of Research in Personality, 11,* 73-82.

Orne, M. (1962). On the social psychology of the psychological experiment: With particular reference to demand characteristics and their implications. *American Psychologist, 17,* 776-783.

Presidential Commission on Obscenity and Pornography. (1970). *Technical reports of the Presidential Commission on Obscenity and Pornography.* Washington, DC: Government Printing Office.

Quinsey, V., Chaplin, T., & Varney, G. (1981). A comparison of rapists' and non-sex offenders' sexual preferences for mutually consenting sex, rape and physical abuse of women. *Behavioral Assessment, 3,* 127-135.

Reage, P. (1965). *Story of O.* New York: Ballantine.

Regina v. Hicklin L.R. 3 Q.B. 360 (1868).

Rosenthal, R., & Rosnow, R. S. (1969). *Artifact in behavioral research.* New York: Academic Press.

Rosenwald, G. C. (1986). Why operationalism doesn't go away: Extrascientific incentives of social-psychological research. *Philosophy of the Social Sciences, 16,* 303-330.

Roth v. United States, 354 U.S. 476 (1957).

Russell, D.E.H. (1988). Pornography and rape: A causal model. *Political Psychology, 9*(1), 41-73.

Sanday, P. R. (1981). The socio-cultural context of rape: A cross-cultural study. *Journal of Social Issues, 37,* 5-27.

Sapolsky, B. S., & Zillman, D. (1981). The effect of soft-core and hard-core erotica on provoked and unprovoked behavior. *Journal of Sex Research, 17,* 319-343.

Schauer, F. F. (1976). *The law of obscenity.* Washington, DC: Bureau of National Affairs.

Schwartz, S. (1973). The effects of sex guilt and sexual arousal on the retention of birth control information. *Journal of Consulting and Clinical Psychology, 41,* 300-305.

Scott, J. (1990). Obscentiy and the law: Is it possible for a jury to apply contemporary community standards in determining obscenity? *Law and Human Behavior, 14*(2), 139-150.

Siebert, F. S., Peterson, T., & Schramm, W. (1956). *Four theories of the press: The authoritarian, libertarian, social responsibility and Soviet communist concepts of what the press should be and do.* Urbana: University of Illinois Press.

Smith, M. D. (1987). The incidence and prevalence of woman abuse in Toronto. *Violence and Victims, 2,* 123-187.

Smith v. U.S. 431 U.S. 291 (1977).

Soble, A. (1986). *Pornography, Marxism, feminism and the future of sexuality.* New Haven, CT: Yale University Press.

Stanley v. Georgia 394 U.S. 557 (1969).

Steinem, G. (1980). Erotica and pornography: A clear and present difference. *Take back the night: Women on pornography* (pp. 35-39). New York: William Morrow.

Tannenbaum, P. H. (1970). Emotional arousal as a mediator of erotic communication effects. *Technical reports of the Presidential Commission on Obscenity and Pornography* (Vol. 8). Washington, DC: Government Printing Office.

Tighe, T. J., & Leaton, R. N. (1976). *Habituation: Perspectives from child development, animal behavior, and neurophysiology.* Hillsdale, NJ: Lawrence Erlbaum.

Walker, C. E. (1970). Erotic stimuli and the aggressive sexual offender. In *Technical reports of the Presidential Commission on Obscenity and Pornography* (Vol. 7). Washington, DC: Government Printing Office.

Webster's Dictionary. (1990). Springfield, MA: Miriam-Webster.

Williams, B. (1979). *Report on the committee on obscenity and film censorship.* London: HMSO.

Wilson, B. J., Linz, D., Donnerstein, E., & Stipp, H. (1992). The impact of social issue television programming on attitudes toward rape. *Human Communication Research, 19*(2), 179-208.

Wurtzel, A., & Lometti, G. (1984). Researching television violence. *Society, 21*(6), 22-30.

Yang, N., & Linz, D. (1990, Spring). Movie ratings and the content of adult videos: The sex violence ratio. *Journal of Communication, 40*(2), 28-42.

Yankelovich, Clancy, & Schulman (1986, July). Pornography: A poll. *Time,* 21-22.

Zillmann, D. (1971). Excitation transfer in communication-mediated aggressive behavior. *Journal of Experimental Social Psychology, 7,* 419-434.

Zillmann, D. (1984). *Victimization of women through pornography.* Proposal to the National Science Foundation. Bloomington: Indiana University.

Zillmann, D. (1986). *Effects of prolonged consumption of pornography.* Paper presented for the Surgeon General's Workshop on Pornography and Public Health, Virginia.

Zillmann, D., & Bryant, J. (1982). Pornography, sexual callousness, and the trivialization of rape. *Journal of Communication, 32,* 10-21.

Zillmann, D., & Bryant, J. (1984). Effects of massive exposure to pornography. In N. M. Malamuth & E. Donnerstein (Eds.), *Pornography and sexual aggression.* New York: Academic Press.

Zillmann, D., & Bryant, J. (1986). *Pornography's impact on sexual satisfaction.* Unpublished manuscript, Indiana University, Bloomington.

Zillmann, D., & Bryant, J. (1988). Effects of prolonged consumption of pornography on family values. *Journal of Family Issues, 9,* 518-544.

Zillmann, D., Bryant, J., & Carveth, R. A. (1981). The effect of erotica featuring sadomasochism and bestiality on motivated intermale aggression. *Personality and Social Psychology Bulletin, 7,* 153-159.

Zillmann, D., Bryant, J., Comisky, P. W., & Medoff, N. J. (1981). Excitation and hedonic valence in the effect of erotica on motivated intermale aggression. *European Journal of Social Psychology, 11,* 233-252.

Zillmann, D., Katcher, A. H., & Milavsky, B. (1972). Excitation transfer from physical exercise to subsequent aggressive behavior. *Journal of Experimental Social Psychology, 8,* 247-259.

Zilllman, D., & Sapolsky, B. S. (1977). What mediates the effect of mild erotica on annoyance and hostile behavior in males? *Journal of Personality and Social Psychology, 35,* 587-596.

Index

Abel, G. G., 32, 48
Adams, S., 52
American Booksellers Association v.
  Hudnut (1986), 14, 50
Arluk, I., 29, 43
Attorney General's Commission on Pornography (1986), 23, 25

Barak, A., 50
Barbaree, H. E., 32, 33
Barlow, D. H., 32
Barnes v. Glen Theatre, Inc. (1991), 8
Baron, L., 18, 19, 34, 50, 51, 57
Baxter, D. J., 33
Beckett, C., 61
Bell, P., 19
Bem, S. L., 53
Bently, B., 52
Ben-Veniste, R., 31, 56
Berger, C., 58
Berkowitz, L., 48, 49
Blackwell, K., 52
Blanchard, E. B., 32
Brandenburg v. Ohio (1969), 30
Brannigan, A., 36, 37, 59, 60
Braucht, G. N., 39
Bross, M., 42
Brownmiller, S., 46
Bryant, J., 16, 17, 20, 21, 22, 23, 25, 26,
  28, 58
Butler v. Queen (1992), 15
Byrne, D., 29, 39, 40

Carveth, R. A., 20
Ceniti, J., 48

Chaffee, S., viii, 58
Chapin, M., 42
Chaplin, T., 32
Check, J. V. P., 42, 46, 47, 48, 51
Christensen, F., 36
Clancy, 38
Comisky, P. W., 16, 20, 58
Cook, R. F., 32
Cowan, G., 54

Daley, P., 52
Davidson, P. R., 33
Davis, K. E., 39
Dawson, M. E., 21
Dietz, S., 52
Dolff, D. J., 36
Donnerstein, E. I., 18, 28, 29, 43, 48, 49,
  52, 55, 61
Downs, D., 30
Dworkin, A., 4, 12

Falwell, J., 7, 50
Feshbach, S., 48
Fisher, W., 40, 60
Fosen, R. H., 32

Garcia, L. T., 41
Gardiner, H. C., 7
Gerrard, M., 40
Gibbons, F. X., 40
Goldenberg, S., 36, 37, 59, 60
Goldstein, M., 31
Gould, L., 7
Gray, S. H., 36, 37

71

Green, R., 31
Griffitt, W., 41
Grings, W. W., 21
Gross, L., 36
Guild, D., 32
Gunther, A., 41

Haber, S., 48
Hawkins, R., viii
Heavy, C., 58
Heilbrun, A. B., 47
Hess, B., 13
Howard, J. L., 38

Intons-Peterson, M. J., 43

Jacobellis v. Ohio (1964), 1
Jarvie, I. C., 36
Johnson, W. T., 31
Judd, C., 53
Judd, L., 31

Kant, H., 31
Katcher, A. H., 18
Kelley, K., 29, 40, 41
Kenny, D. A., 53
Kingsley International Pictures Corp. v.
    Regents (1959), 11
Klein, L., 28
Kogan, N., 41
Krafka, C., 55
Kupperstein, L., 31
Kutchinsky, B., 31, 32, 33, 39, 56

Lahey, K. A., 34
Lamberth, J., 39, 40
Lance, L., 28
Land, K., 28
Lanthier, R. D., 32
Leaton, R. N., 21
Lee, C., 54
Levy, D., 54

Linz, D., vii, 13, 28, 29, 42, 43, 51, 52, 55,
    58, 61, 69
Locke, J., 9
Lometti, G., 36

MacKinnon, C., 12, 45
Malamuth, N. M., vii, 42, 46, 47, 48, 49,
    51, 54, 58, 69
Malcom, P. B., 33
Mann, J., 39
Marshall, W. L., 32, 33
Maslin, J., 52
McKay, H. B., 36
McKenzie-Mohr, D., 53
Medoff, N. J., 16, 20, 58
Memoirs v. Massachusetts (1966), 11
Michael, R. P., 24
Milavsky, B., 18
Miller v. California (1973), 28
Mitchell, H. E., 40
Mosher, D., 39, 40
Mueller, C., 18

O'Brien, M., 54
Obscene Publication Act of 1857, 8
Orne, M., 37

Penrod, S., 13, 52, 55, 61
Peters, J. J., 31
Peterson, T., 6
Presidential Commission on Pornogra-
    phy and Obscenity (1970), 30, 31,
    32, 39

Quinsey, V., 32

Reage, P., 3
Regina, v. Hicklin (1986), 8
Rice, C., 31
Rosenthal, R., 37
Rosenwald, G. C., 37
Roskos-Ewoldsen, B., 43

Rosnow, R. S., 37
Roth v. United States (1957), 8
Russell, D., 61

Sanday, P. R., 47
Sapolsky, B. S., 16, 19, 20, 58
Schramm, W. 6
Schulman, 38
Schwartz, S., 40
Scott, J., 28
Seis, D., 47
Shafer, B., 28
Sidman, J., 39
Siebert, F. S., 6
Smith, M. D., 38
Smith v. United States (1977), 28
Snyder, D., 54
Sobel, A., 36
Starr, S., 39
Steinem, G., 3
Straus, M., 34

Tannenbaum, P. H., 35
Tighe, T. J., 21
Turner, C., 13

Varney, G., 32

Walker, C. E., 31
Williams, B., 36
Wilson, B. J., 29, 31
Wilson, D. W., 18
Wurtzel, A., 36

Yang, N., 51
Yankelovich, 38

Zanna, M., 53
Zillmann, D., 16, 17, 18, 19, 20, 21, 22,
    23, 24, 25, 26, 28, 38, 58
Zumpe, D., 24

About the Authors

Daniel Linz received his Ph.D. in psychology from the University of Wisconsin in 1985 and is currently an Associate Professor in the Department of Communication and Chair of the Law and Society Program at the University of California, Santa Barbara. His work focuses on testing and evaluating the social psychological assumptions embedded in legal policies concerning mass communication including such topics as pretrial publicity, libel, sexual aggression, and violence in the media. He is co-author of the book *The Question of Pornography: Research Findings and Policy Implications* and is author or co-author of more than 50 articles and chapters in communication, psychology, and legal books and journals.

Neil Malamuth (Ph.D., UCLA, 1975) is Professor of Communication and of Psychology and is the Chairman of the Department of Communication at the University of Michigan, Ann Arbor. He has published more than sixty professional articles, primarily on the topics of men's antisocial behavior against women and on pornography. He edited a book titled *Pornography and Sexual Aggression* (with Edward Donnerstein) and a special issue of the *Journal of Social Issues* (with Rowell Huesmann) on the subject of media violence. He is currently Associate Editor of the *Journal of Research in Personality* and serves on the editorial boards of *Communication Research* and the *Journal of Sex Research*. He is also a member of the National Institute of Mental Health's (NIMH) committee that reviews grant proposals in the areas of violence and of traumatic stress. He has testified on the subject of pornography before various national and foreign government commissions, including presenting testimony on behalf of the American Psychological Association before joint hearings of the U.S. Senate and Congress. In an objective analysis of eminence in social psychology that appeared in the 1992 issue of *Personality and Social Psychology Bulletin*, he was one of seven researchers ranked in the top 100 scholars across all of the four measures of eminence used in this study. Formerly, he was on the faculty of the University of California, Los Angeles, and the University of Manitoba, Canada.